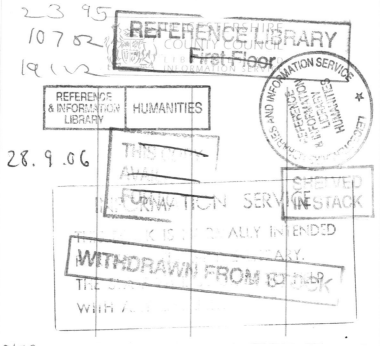

A Call to Live:
Vocation for Everyone

Steve Walton was a Vocation and Ministry Adviser with CPAS from 1986 to 1992. He is a Church of England clergyman, currently completing research work on the New Testament. A former UCCF travelling secretary, he has been both a speaker and a counsellor at Spring Harvest. He is an experienced speaker, reviewer, and writer who also referees volleyball at the highest level in England. He lives in Bedford with his wife, Ali.

A CALL TO LIVE
Vocation for Everyone

STEVE WALTON

TRi△NGlE

First published 1994

Triangle
Society for Promoting Christian Knowledge
Holy Trinity Church
Marylebone Road
London NW1 4DU

The Scripture quotations are usually taken from the *New
Revised Standard Version* of the Bible, © 1989 by the
Division of Christian Education of the National Council of
Churches of Christ in the USA, and are used by permission.
Where I have used other versions or my own translation I
have acknowledged this.

British Library Cataloguing-in-Publication Data
A catalogue record for this book is available from the British
Library.

ISBN 0–281–04771–5

Typeset by Dorwyn Ltd, Rowlands Castle, Hants
Printed and bound in Great Britain by
BPC Paperbacks Ltd
Member of British Printing Company Ltd

To Di Lammas,
colleague, sister and friend

Contents

Preface   ix

1   Vocation?   1

2   'Call' in the New Testament   13

3   Called to Belong   27

4   Called to Be   44

5   Called to Let God Be God   59

6   Called to Do   74

7   Called to Work   86

8   How to Recover Calling   100

Notes   116

Resources for Further Thought and Action   121

Portraits

Preface

The lack of a thought-out, biblically based understanding of 'call' and 'vocation' in our day has for some years been one of the great gaps in Christian writing. I spent six years working in the 'vocation' field, advising and helping those considering ordained ministry in the Church of England, and found myself continually frustrated by the lack of a clear, non-technical, study of the theme of 'call' that I could suggest to those I met. I was therefore very interested when the idea of this book was put to me, believing that the potential for releasing Christian people into service for Christ through the multi-dimensional view of 'call' found in the New Testament is enormous. It is my hope and prayer that God will use this book to that end.

I owe a considerable debt to a number of people who have helped my thinking on this topic. This debt is evident from the notes and the suggestions for further thought and action. Others kindly gave time to discuss ideas with me, especially Tom Frank (then Chairman of the Association of Graduate Careers Advisory Services), Sir Timothy Hoare (Career Plan), Roy McCloughry (The Kingdom Trust), Dr Richard Higginson (Ethics Lecturer at Ridley Hall, Cambridge, and Director of the Ridley Hall Foundation), Graham Dow (Bishop of Willesden), and Elaine Storkey (Director, Christian Impact).

I was glad of the opportunity to speak to groups using much of the material in this book, particularly the ACCM (now ABM) Vocations Advisers' Conference, the Oxford diocesan post-ordination training group, two Summer

Schools for St John's Extension Studies, and the participants in numerous CPAS 'You and the Ministry' weekends.

I am particularly grateful to those who read the book in
manuscript and made a number of helpful comments:
Robert Penman (Chairman, Arts Centre Group), Dr
Richard Higginson, Dr Christopher Cunliffe (Vocations
Officer, Advisory Board of Ministry), James Ambrose and
Di Lammas (Vocation and Ministry Advisers, CPAS). It is
considerably better for their feedback, but they should not,
of course, be held responsible for any of its remaining
weaknesses.

The encouragement and support of my wife, Ali,
throughout the work on the book have meant more than I
can say. I have also appreciated very much the courtesy,
helpfulness, and hard work of the staff at Triangle Books,
especially my editor, Rachel Boulding.

Whilst on the CPAS staff I had the very great privilege of
working alongside Di Lammas for six years, and she has
been the sounding board and stimulus for much in this
book. In recognition of her support, help and encouragement, this book is dedicated to her.

Steve Walton
The Feast of the Conversion of St Paul, 1994

1 *Vocation?*

Eric had worked for the brick company in the kilns for twenty years, ever since he left school, when he was called into the office one day. To his surprise and horror he was told that he would be made redundant at the end of the following month. When he asked why this was happening, he was told that there was a down-turn in the building industry and therefore the firm's bricks weren't selling. Some of the workers had to be 'let go' and he was one of the unlucky ones. Eric was shell-shocked, but went home and told his family the bad news. Later, he went to ask his church minister's advice about how to decide what to do next. What advice should the minister offer?

Clare is thirteen and having to make her choices of subjects for public examinations when she is sixteen. These choices will be important, since the future directions she could go will in some measure be determined by them. Clare is a member of the young people's group in her church and asks her youth leader how being a Christian should make a difference to her choices. How can she find out what God wants her to do? What should the youth leader suggest to her?

Graham is employed by a newsagent, but when he was in his early twenties he found himself increasingly drawn into local politics. With the support of his local party he stood in a by-election and was elected as a local councillor. Because Graham is a Christian he thinks a good deal about how to apply his faith to the political arena. However, as time has passed, Graham has found himself facing more and more difficult choices, where the party line seems to him to go against what he sees as the implications of his Christian convictions. After thinking things over for some time he talks to the members of his church house group and asks for their prayers, since he has now begun to feel that politics may not be for him at all. How should Graham think this through and decide whether he should resign as a councillor? How can he decide what God wants in all this?

Nancy is single and has recently retired after over forty years in her secretarial job. She greatly enjoyed her job and now feels unsure about what to do with her time. She is very fit and active and is looking forward to using her retirement for getting her garden in order, but wonders if there are other things she should be doing. She is a long-standing church member and wants to be useful to God in her retirement. How should she decide what to be doing?

Chris has been a vicar for five years and is surprised one day when a young couple, Ken and Sally, ask to come and see him. When they meet, Ken explains that they are wondering whether God is calling them to serve in missionary work overseas. They feel increasingly uneasy in the highly affluent lifestyle that they enjoy because of Ken's work in the financial sector. What questions should Chris raise with them, and what advice should he offer?

WHAT IS 'VOCATION'?

What kind of person picks up a book about 'vocation'? All five of the people above are asking questions that are, in one sense or other, vocational. We shall return to each of them at different stages of this book to see what our study of 'vocation' has to offer to their situations.

But what is 'vocation', or its companion, 'call'? The English word 'call' comes to us from Greek, the language of the New Testament, whereas 'vocation' comes to us from Latin. Both were originally used in a range of ways, from speaking to someone ('he called to her') to more abstract uses ('she called upon the gods'). Such uses have the idea of *communication* at their heart, usually spoken communication.

The modern world uses both call and vocation with a wide variety of meanings and, in order to clarify what this book is about, we need to look over the range of understandings that are around.

IDEAS OF VOCATION

Some people use 'vocation' mainly of jobs or careers. Thus government agencies speak of 'vocational training', by which they mean training people so that they are more likely to fit into the slots available in the job market. Or some specific professions (and they are usually *professions*) are described as 'vocations', such as teaching or various forms of medical work. Describing these types of work as 'vocations' usually implies that the people following those 'callings' do it out of a commitment to serve the community or their fellow human beings. In this sense the word can sometimes be used as a lever, perhaps to persuade teachers that they should settle for a lower salary because theirs is a 'vocation'. The assumption is that people whose jobs are seen as vocations will enjoy greater job satisfaction.

The Christian world has its own particular use of call and vocation. The claim that is made when speaking of 'call' – that there is a God who does the calling – is taken seriously among Christians. However, the good that this does is often *un*done by restricting the use of call to a small group of people. So clergy, missionaries, monks and nuns are all described as people with *callings*, while everyone else has *jobs*. The idea is that God specifically calls those who are to serve in church-type work, with the implication that others should not expect such an experience.

When you ask where the idea that God only calls those in 'Christian work' comes from, people often point to the Bible, to the stories of God calling someone to a particular task: Moses, Samuel, Isaiah, Amos or Paul, for example. These stories are particularly striking examples of God intervening to change the direction of someone's life. Some people also point to great heroes from church history who have experienced such a call. In the fourth century Augustine of Hippo, who had led a dissolute life as a young man, heard a voice in a garden in Milan telling him to take and read a book he saw, which turned out to be Paul's letter to the Romans. John Wesley in the eighteenth century, having preached about Christ in America without sensing that he truly knew Christ personally, felt his heart to be 'strangely warmed' within him as he heard Martin Luther's preface to the same letter to the Romans read aloud in a meeting in Aldersgate Street, London. The 'Cambridge Seven' in Victorian times were extremely able Cambridge graduates who went to China as missionaries, among them C. T. Studd, who left a glittering cricketing career behind. In the twentieth century, David Wilkerson, the Pentecostal pastor, felt drawn to work among gangs in New York in the late 1950s. Such are the kind of examples that spring to many Christians' minds when they hear the word 'call'.

THE WORLD OF WORK

Each of these uses of 'call' has real benefits as well as not a few drawbacks, which we will look at shortly. First, though, the other key context for thinking about vocation today is the world of work, a world that is very different from twenty, or even ten, years ago. Christians have long believed, rightly, that people's main occupations should provide one of the key areas of fulfilment in their lives, whether (for example) in paid work, or as a homemaker and parent. But the world in which that search for fulfilment takes place has changed dramatically.

Today there is a *scramble for security*, which results from the pressure produced by not having a regular income. During the recession in the West in the early 1990s there have been examples of employees taking no pay rise, or even a drop in pay, in order to keep their jobs. In Britain the growth in repossessions of houses because people could not keep up their mortgage payments has made many extremely cautious about rocking the boat at all in industrial relations, because it is their jobs that will be on the line.

The growing materialism of the West puts people under pressure to have more money so that they can get the things that the advertisers tell them that they cannot do without. This is particularly noticeable with children and adolescents, who swallow the line that they must have a particular brand of trainers or whatever and then tell their parents that they will be ridiculed if they don't. The result is more pressure on the parents.

A second mark of the world of work today is the *pressure for 'commitment'*. Employers demand more for the wage that they pay. This can also affect recruitment of new staff. A firm was giving a Sunday presentation to prospective workers in a university town, and thick snow fell on Saturday night. One student who failed to go to the presentation, because he was not able to get into the town as a result of the snow, was told that the company would not be taking the interviews any further, because he 'lacked commitment'. Professionals have long worked excessive hours because of the understanding that promotion goes to those who show their commitment by working late, and this is increasingly so throughout the world of work. When an organization can pick and choose its staff, it can impose these demands.

Some employers seek to own their staff body and soul. This can put pressures on a person's integrity. One young Christian man in the building industry found himself being told to provide invoices which charged very considerably higher rates than should have been the case; he resisted the pressure to be less than honest, but could easily have found himself out of work by doing so.

A third factor today is the *need to succeed*. In many spheres the only way is up; if you are satisfied with the level you have reached, you may be seen as dispensable when the next job cuts have to be made. Employers look for those with get up and go, with energy. The result of this for some churches is that they cannot find people to lead their children's groups or house groups, to attend the prayer meetings regularly, or to be involved in the local community, because the need to succeed has become all-important: all the people who might do those things are busy working late or working shifts.

There is, of course, a balance to be found in this, for it is clearly vital that some Christian people should be at the heart of the nation's commercial and industrial life, influencing things in a just and honest direction, both as workers and management. The pressure in some churches to show your 'commitment' by turning up to every meeting that is held, militates against allowing Christians to get seriously involved in union affairs or senior management – as well as more widely in local politics, school governorships, and many more areas. Members of a local church will need to work together in seeking the appropriate sphere for each of them to serve God, and it will be vital for each to respect and trust those Christians whose sphere of service is different from their own.

Along with these pressures, for many Christian people there is a *radical split between life at work and life in church*. What goes on in church seems light years away from their daily experience. The illustrations of the Christian life in the sermons they hear are about missionaries, ministers or biblical characters, not men and women from the world they inhabit. The prayers they pray in church may rarely relate to the world in which they work, being focused on missionary work, church events and sick people, rather than industry, parenting, or school, for example. The feeling can grow up that Christian faith is fine for your personal life, but irrelevant for work and society: 'privately engaging, but socially irrelevant', as Os Guinness puts it.

PROBLEMS WITH THIS PICTURE
The picture I have described results in several problems, both for the individuals concerned and for their families, churches, and those who pastor them.

One instant result of the near worship of work in modern Western society is the marginalization of many people, particularly those not in paid work at any time. This clearly means those called 'unemployed', but includes home-makers, full-time parents, and retired people too. Such people receive the impression that they are not valued because they do not produce money. This impression is no less strong in many churches, where the major reaction to people who are unwaged is to try to help them find paid work or sometimes voluntary work until they can find paid work. Those who stay at home to bring up children – usually, but not always, women – can feel undervalued by their churches.

With this impression goes another, that the 'really committed' Christian is the one who is ordained, or in missionary work, or the like. These are the people who are prayed for regularly, who are held up as models of the Christian life in sermons, and who young people are encouraged to emulate. Business-people earning large salaries can get the feeling that their main purpose as Christians is to give a proportion of their salary to their church or to Christian missionary work; for the rest of the time they are second-class Christians.

Along with these difficulties goes a model of how God guides his people that does not reflect the experience of most Christians. In the autumn of 1993 there was some debate in England about an Anglican priest who published a book explaining how he had arrived at a 'non-realist' account of Christian faith.[1] The author had come to believe that God is not objectively real and 'out there', but rather that 'God' is the label we give to our ideals: we believe in God in the same way that we believe in justice, for example.

What was interesting in this debate was the reaction to this view. It led to people saying that the idea of a God who regularly intervenes in the world (which these people took to be the picture of God in the Bible) has been incredible for years. It is not, in fact, what most church members believe. Here is another point at which many Christians find their life outside the Christian community to be radically different from their life within the fellowship of the church. Their daily experience is not that they regularly meet bushes that are burning but not being consumed, nor that they often have great visions of God when sitting in a church building on their own. God seems to be different in their experience from the situation that they understand to be the norm in the Bible.

This difference stems partly from a mistaken approach to the events described in the Bible, for they are recorded precisely because they were unusual. It was not that every Israelite had experiences like those of Moses or Isaiah. Rather, God gave those experiences to such people because they were part of his purpose to reveal himself. 'Normal' Christian living is to be found in the run-of-the-mill existence of the average Israelite or Christian, as far as we can understand it, not in the abnormal encounters with God of a Moses or an Isaiah. Indeed, if God were to intervene constantly in dramatic ways, our individual humanity and accountability to God would be overridden. (We shall think more about how God guides his people in chapters 5 and 6.)

That is not to say that Christians today *never* have meetings with God like these unusual ones. God is able to do such things and sometimes does. But they should not be held up as the norm for day-to-day Christian living; these unusual experiences are precisely that – unusual.

A consequence of this 'interventionist' view of guidance is that it is very difficult indeed to deal with periods when God does not appear to be saying anything specific to an individual. This becomes particularly acute when the individual concerned wants to know God's will on a specific issue or decision. If the expectation is that God's guidance will always be clear, such an experience can lead to a crisis, even to questioning whether there is a God at all.

The silence of God can also be problematic for a highly rational and cerebral approach to God's guidance. Some Christians react against the interventionist view by arguing that the main means God uses to guide people is the application of their minds to the issue in hand, whether it is to do with a decision about a job, marriage to a particular person, or more usual, day-to-day decisions. Some who hold this view seem to believe that the mind is the *only* means by which God guides people today. Naturally, the mind is important for the Christian life, for our rationality is given to us by God, but our minds are not God. By definition God is wiser than us and sees the whole picture, whereas our view is partial and incomplete. There are therefore limits to how far our minds can take us. From a purely rational perspective, truth is not tidy but messy.

Between the limits of over-rationalism and extreme interventionism lies a position which takes seriously God's creation of us both as rational beings and as beings dependent on him. Both these facets of our humanness need to be expressed in seeking God's guidance.

This leads to a final problem that we need to note, the mistaken desire for complete answers in this life. There is a strong temptation amongst Christian people to want to understand everything in this life, a temptation that is increased by living in a society where eternity and heaven are not on the agenda at all. John White makes this point well:

We Christians are visually handicapped. Our perspective is distorted. Bombarded from all sides with false values, living perpetually among people whose goals are material prosperity, security, pleasure, prestige, it is inevitable that we absorb the atmosphere around us until heaven seems remote while the here and now looms large in our thinking. The future comes to mean tomorrow, next week, ten years from now. We are like people looking at curved mirrors in a fun house, but unlike the crowd laughing at the grotesque images, we see the grotesque as normal! It does not amuse us. We base our lives on it.[2]

The result of this distortion is that Christian people so often want to know *why* something has happened, when in this life such answers are very unlikely. People's desires for meaning, order and happiness can so easily become focused on this life, whereas the God of the Bible cannot be limited in that way, for he inhabits eternity and his ways are higher than ours.[3]

BACK TO THE BIBLE

In the light of this breadth of views of vocation and calling, we shall go back to the Bible to seek the roots of a Christian understanding of vocation there. This will necessarily involve thinking about guidance, the nature of the God of the Bible, and the way he relates to his creation. This will lead us to think about the purposes of God for the universe, and for Christians as a body and individually, as Scripture explains them. In that context we shall be able to see how Christians down the years have lived out the teaching of the Bible, and to reflect on what it might mean for us today.

In this study the use of our minds in reading and thinking about Scripture will be vital. God's purpose in creating us as thinking, rational creatures was not a plot to tempt us to rebel against him by using our minds; there is a right Christian use of the mind in submission to God's revelation of himself. This can be seen in the creation story in Genesis 1, where God tells the man and the woman, 'Be fruitful and multiply, and fill the earth and subdue it; and have dominion over the fish of the sea and over the birds of the air and over every living thing that moves upon the earth.'[4] The responsibility of humankind for the created world implies the need to *understand* the world. It was this perspective that led to 'Great are the works of the Lord, studied by all who delight in them'[5] being carved above the door of the Cavendish Laboratory in Cambridge. The scientists of the day saw their work as 'thinking God's thoughts after him', and their minds were applied to the world, not in arrogance, believing that God would vanish when they really understood why things are as they are, but in humility, seeking to carry out the mandate of Genesis 1 to 'subdue the earth'.

Our minds have an important place in our lives with God. Christians ought not to be people who switch off their brains when they begin to follow Jesus, but people who apply Christ-centred thinking to every area of life.

LINES OF APPROACH
In going back to the Bible we shall look carefully at the use of the 'call' word group in the New Testament. We shall group the uses into four main categories, which will then open up practical questions of how we work these ideas out today. In each case there will be exercises to try, to help in taking forward the principles highlighted by each aspect of 'call'.

In the New Testament we meet the verb translated 'to call', the noun 'calling' and the adjective 'called', as well as two interesting specific verbs, 'to call to oneself' and 'to call upon'. In total there are some 228 uses of the various words. Our study will focus on uses of the word group where God or Jesus Christ is the one doing the calling, directly or indirectly; we will leave aside uses where human beings are doing the calling.

For Reflection
How do I understand the meaning of the words 'call' and 'vocation'? In what ways do I believe that God has called me?

2 'Call' in the New Testament

There are various understandings of 'call' and 'vocation' around on the modern scene. In this chapter we shall be thinking about the New Testament's use of 'call' by looking at Paul's letter to the Romans, which contains the four major uses of the word.

> Paul, a servant of Jesus Christ, *called to be* an apostle, set apart for the gospel of God, which he promised beforehand through his prophets in the holy scriptures, the gospel concerning his Son, who was descended from David according to the flesh and was declared to be Son of God with power according to the spirit of holiness by resurrection from the dead, Jesus Christ our Lord, through whom we have received grace and apostleship to bring about the obedience of faith among all the Gentiles for the sake of his name, including yourselves who are *called to belong* to Jesus Christ.
> To all God's beloved in Rome, who are *called to be* saints. (Romans 1.1–7; my italics)

In later chapters we will look in more detail at each of the four major senses of the word that we shall find, focusing on how we can work out those key biblical ideas today. But first we need to recognize those four main uses of 'call'.

CALLED TO BELONG

For Paul, and the other New Testament writers, this was the main use of the word: Paul writes, 'yourselves who are *called to belong to Jesus Christ*'. When someone comes to faith in Christ, it is God who has made the first move. He has issued the invitation, he has *called* them. It was not that the person woke up one morning and thought that getting to know God might be a good idea, but rather that God took the initiative. He began to speak to the person, to call them into a relationship with himself. Our seeking God is always a response to God having sought us.

This happens in many different ways for different people. For some it is a particular event that sparks them off to look for God, such as a bereavement, the birth of a child, a broken relationship or moving to a new area. For many it is a friendship with someone who is already a believer. For others it is reading a book, perhaps the Bible itself. There are many means that God uses to issue his invitation.

The *content* of the invitation is summed up by Paul in the first few verses of Romans, for it is through the Christian gospel, the message, that God issues his invitation. When someone starts to think about God and to look for him, it is this message that they will need to hear. We shall therefore review the main themes of the gospel message as Paul explains it in these verses, so that we in turn can grasp the essentials of the message we pass on to those seeking God in our day. Paul summarizes his message in two affirmations: it is the gospel of God and it is the gospel concerning his Son.

The gospel of God

Paul begins his letter to the Roman Church by underlining that his message is not a human invention, but comes from God himself. In the rest of the letter Paul goes on to unfold his understanding of the message. He emphasizes a similar point in writing to the strife-torn churches of Galatia:

> For I want you to know, brothers and sisters, that the gospel that was proclaimed by me is not of human origin; for I did not receive it from a human source, nor

was I taught it, but I received it by a revelation of Jesus Christ. (Galatians 1.11–12)

Graham Greene's novel *The Third Man*, set in Vienna after the Second World War, tells the story of Harry Lime (a fictional character, although Greene based his account on real events). Lime was infamous as a seller of black-market penicillin. The trouble was that his penicillin had been mixed with other things to make it stretch further. So when people used the penicillin they had bought from him, it was not effective in treating their diseases and infections. By mixing it with other things, he had destroyed its effectiveness. So it is with the Christian gospel. Because it is from God, it will be powerful and effective in leading us to a new relationship with God. But dilute it with other ideas and you will destroy its power.

Our responsibility today for the message is therefore twofold. First we must receive it ourselves. We do this by turning from our old way of life, when we lived independently of God, and welcoming God into our lives as the one we will serve from now on. Second, we must pass the message on without addition or subtraction, both by living it out and by speaking of it to others. We will consider later what these mean in day-to-day practical terms.

The gospel concerning his Son
Paul's other affirmation is that the gospel is all about Jesus Christ. It is not first and foremost about us human beings, although it has vital things to say to our human situation – it is about Christ. Paul focuses on four crucial truths about Jesus in these verses.

Jesus is both God and human. Jesus is God's Son, but born in human flesh. Because of our rebellion against God, we needed a bridge to be built between God and us. A bridge, by definition, needs to touch both sides of the chasm it is crossing. Jesus had to be both human and divine, for only that way could he bridge the gap between God and us.

His divinity is the reason that Jesus has power to save both Paul and us from the egotism and self-centredness in which we human beings live our lives. Human beings, however good, cannot deliver themselves from themselves. Because Jesus is God, he has the power to deliver us all – indeed, to restore the whole universe to God's original purposes for it.

Jesus' birth as a human being also means that he is a figure of real, dateable history. He really existed. The Christian faith is not based on unhistorical legends, but is rooted in God having become one of us in a particular place at a particular time. Christian claims about Jesus are in principle testable by historical enquiry. There are clearly limits to how much a historian can check about Jesus, as with any figure of the past. But at the points where the New Testament portrait of Jesus can be checked against the data of archaeology and ancient history, it has come out with a clean bill of health over and over again.

Jesus was descended from David. This may not seem very relevant to us twentieth-century Christians, but that shows how little we know of the roots of our faith, particularly its Jewish and Old Testament roots. Through the Old Testament prophets, God had been promising that he would send someone, sometimes called the Messiah, to save his people. This man would be a descendant of King David, perhaps the greatest king in the history of Israel – 'great David's greater Son', as the hymn puts it. As a result it was important to Paul – who like most of the earliest Christians was born a Jew – that Jesus was descended from David. Had he not been, he could not have done the work of the Messiah, saving God's people.

The statement that Jesus was 'descended from David' tells us something else, for it means that God had prepared for his coming for centuries. The Old Testament Scriptures are full of God's promises of this one whom he promised to send, from the time of Moses. It was not that God was taken by surprise when his good intentions for the first people were spoilt by their disobedience (the story is in Genesis 3). It was not that God suddenly had to rethink, because his 'Plan A' had gone wrong, and so he came up with 'Plan B', which was that he would send Jesus. No. God knew from the outset that humankind would need delivering, and planned from eternity to send his own Son to do it. More than that, God prepared for the coming of his Son both by telling the Israelite prophets about him and by giving the people of Israel pictures and models of what Jesus would accomplish, such as their sacrificial system.

God's purpose to deliver us goes back before time existed, and has been promised in the Scriptures. We are tied by this purpose of God to history in a way that encourages us here, for we can see that God prepared the way carefully for the coming of his Son.

Jesus died and rose from the dead. Paul describes Jesus as the one who did what no one else has done, for he defeated death on Easter morning. Christians believe that the events of that weekend in Jerusalem are the most significant events in the whole of history, for through the dying and rising again of Jesus we were delivered from our self-centredness and set free to live as the people God intended us to be.

It is worth noting the proportions of the four New Testament Gospels that are given over to the events of the death and resurrection of Jesus: each of them gives between a third and a half of their books to this period of a week. Matthew, Mark, Luke, and John were not writing biographies in the modern sense, where every part of the person's life receives coverage, but they were writing *Gospels*, books that proclaimed the facts of who Jesus is and what he has achieved. That is why they focus so much on his death and resurrection.

The lesson of focusing on what the death and resurrection of Jesus mean for us is one we easily forget. That is surely one reason for Jesus giving us the communion service (or eucharist, which means 'thanksgiving') to remind us again and again of the need to keep our attention on his death for us. The Christian life is to be shaped by the cross and resurrection of Jesus Christ: we follow in the way of the cross, which is a way of suffering, and we follow in the way of the resurrection, which is a way of ultimate glory.

Jesus is Lord. Jesus rose from the dead, and that is why Paul is so sure that Jesus is now Lord of the universe. God declared him victorious by the resurrection, just as the referee raises the winning boxer's arm at the end of a fight. God declared that Christ rules the universe, and we therefore need to live under his rule in obedience.

The New Testament knows nothing of the idea that we can accept the good things that flow from the death and resurrection of Jesus – forgiveness, friendship with God, new life, the promise of life beyond the grave, and many more – without being ready to live in submission to his rule. In a previous generation, some Christians mistakenly spoke of becoming a Christian as accepting Jesus *purely* as Saviour. They regarded accepting him as *Lord* as a step to be taken later, when Christians gave themselves whole-heartedly to obeying what Christ wanted. Christians who taught this view seemed to believe that it was possible to receive the good things that Jesus' death makes available (accepting Jesus as Saviour) without a simultaneous commitment to serve Christ and put him first as Lord. But Jesus is called 'Saviour' only eighteen times in the New Testament, and 'Lord' 288 times. This balance shows that the first Christians understood that to accept the good things God gives through Jesus also means living under his rule.

The great change in becoming a Christian is the change from 'me first' living to 'Jesus first' living. This is the meaning of repentance, the word often used in describing becoming a Christian. To repent involves turning from living with myself at the centre of my life, which is my natural state, to living with Christ at the centre. It therefore entails a shift from a view that I can manage my own life perfectly well without God, to accepting that I cannot do it alone and need God's power. It means submitting my desires to God's. Instead of what *I* want being the deciding factor in everything, the critical question becomes what *Christ* wants.

This is the central thrust of the questions put to candidates (or parents and godparents) in an Anglican baptism service. They are asked, 'Do you turn to Christ?' and 'Do you repent of your sins?' These are precisely the two sides of becoming a Christian believer, for they are about turning *from* myself as the centre of my life – repenting of my sins – and turning *to* Christ as the centre. Someone who wants the good things Christ offers but who is not willing to put him first, is not ready for commitment to Christ.

It is through this message, a message from God and centred on Jesus Christ, that God calls people from the death of their self-centredness to new life with him. The first Christians heard this call and responded, just as we need to today.

CALLED TO BE

Paul writes that the Christians at Rome are 'called to be saints'. In fact, the original Greek is a phrase with a double meaning. It could be translated 'called to be saints' or it could be translated 'called to be holy'. My guess is that Paul, who was a master of the Greek language, understood the double meaning and probably intended both senses to be heard by the Roman Christians. Both senses are important in thinking about the New Testament understanding of 'call'.

Called to be holy

'Holy' is a word that is often misunderstood today because of its use for special people, special places and the like. The Greek word used means 'set apart': something or someone is 'holy' if they are marked out in a particular way or are earmarked for a particular purpose. The word was first used of God himself, whom the people of Israel learned was quite separate and distinct from them. He was good, they were not. He was pure, they were not. He was just, they were not. He was merciful, they were not. He was perfect, they were not. All these things were summed up in saying God was *holy*.

God's intention, moreover, was that his people should be like him. He told them, 'be holy, for I am holy'.[1] He wanted his people to be distinctive in the world because their lives reflected his own character. The people of Israel, in the Old Testament, were to stand out from the other nations because they lived out the justice and mercy that were in the heart of God himself. The Christian Church, in the New Testament, was to be seen to be distinctive. As Peter wrote, 'Conduct yourselves honourably among the Gentiles, so that, though they may malign you as evildoers, they may see your honourable deeds and glorify God when he comes to judge.'[2]

It is this sense of holiness, of reflecting the character of God in the way that we live, that is important here. Christian people need to be those who live out the faith they profess in their daily lives. If we do that, we will stand out as distinctive people who show compassion, mercy and patience, as those who treat the marginalized of our society with the love which God himself has for them.

This is an area that needs considerable further thought, for it is easy either to be overwhelmed by the needs of the world or to become indifferent to the starving children on our television news every night. It is easy to let the world squeeze us into its own mould (as J. B. Phillips so memorably paraphrased Romans 12.1). But God's call is a call to live distinctively, to let our lights shine in a dark world.

Called to be saints

'Saint' is a word that we have a very good chance of misunderstanding today, for it has become associated with special people, known for their outstanding Christian lives. When the word 'saint' is used, most will think of people like Paul or Mary Magdalene, Francis or Clare, or, in modern times, Mother Teresa or Martin Luther King – Christians who stand out. The New Testament's use of the word contrasts in two ways with this way of thinking: first, 'saint' is simply another word for 'Christian'; and secondly, it is always in the plural, 'saints'. (The apparent exception is Philippians 4.21, 'Greet *every* saint', which is hardly an exception!)

This means that the distinctive, holy life style, which we have already briefly considered, is to be the norm of Christian living. It is not just for super-Christians, but is the expected standard for us all. It is not that, as is sometimes implied, there are two standards of Christian living: a very high standard for Christian leaders and missionaries and a much lower one for the rest of us. Rather, there is one standard of Christian living which is to be the aim of us all.

The fact that the New Testament virtually always uses 'saints' in the plural, is important in providing a corrective to the excessive individualism found in much modern Western thinking about the Christian life. The Christian life in the New Testament contains essential corporate dimensions, whereas many Western Christians speak of '*my* Christian life', '*my* prayer life', 'making *my* communion' and even '*my* church'. Such people treat the New Testament letters as though they were written to individual Christians, and forget that they were written to churches.

The earliest Christians saw themselves as a body of people bound together by Christ. They therefore had responsibilities for bearing one another's burdens, for supporting one another and encouraging one another in faith. They would have been baffled by many modern churches, where people dash into services, talk to no one and then leave without speaking to anyone. When my wife and I once moved to a new area, we visited a few of the churches. After visiting one such church twice, no one had spoken to either of us. The corporate dimensions of the Christian life are vital, and yet so often missing today.

These corporate dimensions are part of God's call for us, according to Paul. They are not an optional extra to the Christian life, for those who like that kind of thing. There is no concept of the 'Lone Ranger' Christian in the New Testament. Rather, the Christian life is a life of *inter*dependence, not *in*dependence.

CALLED TO LET GOD BE GOD

For this use of 'call' we need to look to another part of the letter to the Romans:

> For those whom [God] foreknew he also predestined to be conformed to the image of his Son, in order that he might be the firstborn within a large family. And those whom he predestined he also called; and those whom he called he also justified; and those whom he justified he also glorified. (Romans 8.29–30)

Paul is confident that God will complete the work he has begun in the lives of his people. This comes through vividly in the way he writes, describing Christians as people whom God has foreknown, predestined, called, and justified, using the past tense in each case, for the experience of the Roman Christians was that all these things had already happened to them. God knew them in eternity and chose them to belong to him. He called them to faith when they heard about Jesus Christ. He declared them 'not guilty' and accepted them as members of his people. All these things were past.

The surprise is that Paul goes on to describe the Roman Christians as *glorified*, again using the past tense, implying that they were already fully experiencing glorification. Paul seems to be saying that his sisters and brothers in Rome were already perfected, already enjoying heaven in its fullness, for that is the meaning of being glorified. A moment's thought would have told them – and us – that this was not yet true. Yes, they experienced something of glorification now, in their adoption as children of God, in their present experience of the Holy Spirit's work in their lives, and in many other ways. But they were not yet experiencing the whole, for they were not yet fully perfected. They still disobeyed God. They still hurt their fellow Christians. They still fell ill and died. Yet Paul is so certain that God will bring the Roman Christians to perfection in heaven that he can write as though the transformation is already complete, using the past tense *glorified*. Paul is stretching the boundaries of human language to express this.

Where does his certainty come from? Clearly not from a particular conviction about the Christians to whom he wrote, for Paul was under no illusions about the fallibility of Christian people in this life. He understood that we fail God and do wrong. Paul's confidence sprang from God himself. It was because *God* was at work that Paul could be sure that the task would be completed. That is why he goes on to write, 'If God is for us, who can be against us?'[3] Paul assured his fellow Christians that they could be confident of heaven because God was committed to finishing his work – a work begun back in eternity, when he chose them to be his own, and continued in history, when they heard God's call and were accepted into God's people through his Son. God will complete this work in bringing Christians to be glorified.

The confidence we can have that God, who called us to faith in Jesus Christ, will bring us finally to glory has important implications for the way we think about call.

Because bringing us to glory is ultimately God's work, we need to be people who seek to live his way. This will involve actively looking for what his purposes are to be. It will mean seeking what he is about and being part of that, rather than making our plans and asking God to bless them. We need to aim at living actively under the sovereign power of God.

CALLED TO DO

Finally there is the call to particular tasks or roles, although it is the question many modern Christians ask first. Paul describes himself as 'called to be an apostle', showing that he saw his particular place in God's purposes as one assigned by God himself.

This is an unusual use of 'call' in the New Testament, although it is the commonest use of the word today, such as when we speak of being 'called to the ordained ministry' or 'called to be a missionary'. In fact, out of over 200 New Testament uses of the 'call' word group, only four are to do with the call to a particular task or role. We shall look in detail at those four uses in chapter 6, but observe now that one aspect of 'call' is that it is God's purpose for certain people to serve him in particular ways. Thus seeking and finding God's purposes for each of us is crucial to our life as Christians – and this search will be conducted alongside, and in co-operation with, our brother and sister Christians.

This has implications, too, for Christian thinking about work. How far can we see the tasks and roles of paid employment as a calling in a damaged, imperfect, fallen world? How should we think about those whose work is unpaid, such as home-makers and full-time parents? How far should we expect fulfilment in our daily work, whether paid or not? How should we face, or help others to face, a long or short period of being unwaged?

These are all enormous questions. However, because Paul regards his 'work' as an apostle as a specific calling from God, it should be possible to think Christianly about the connections between 'call' and work, although, as we shall see, the two are never identified as the same thing in the New Testament.

A THREE-STOREY BUILDING

The four uses of 'call' can be seen as four layers of a building process. The call to belong to Jesus Christ is the foundation for the others, for until a person has heard and responded to this call, the other questions about call will not be asked; he or she will be living without access to God, who is the source of calling.

The ground floor is the twin call to holiness and to a corporate life. The call to be holy is critically important to finding more of the purposes of God for us, for disobeying God means that our lives are closed to him. We cannot knowingly continue to disobey God in one area of our lives and then expect the other areas of our lives to be open to him. Seeking true holiness is crucial to living within the call of God for us.

The same is true of the call to be part of the body of Christ, the church. We cannot expect to find more of the calling of God for our lives, whether broadly or narrowly defined, if we ignore the principal means that God has given to help us with that search – his people. A vital part of Christian living is commitment to the people of God, to living in real interdependence with our fellow Christians.

The second storey of the building is the call to let God be God, the call to live actively under the sovereign power of God. It is in pursuing holiness with other Christians that we shall be enabled to depend on God in a way that leads us to seek *his* purposes, to live lives which put his concerns and his purposes at the top of the agenda.

Finally comes the top storey, the call to do, to take on particular tasks or roles. This is dependent on the levels below, just as the top floor of a building could not stay in place without the lower floors and the foundations. To ask questions about how we are to serve God in the narrow sense of 'vocation' without first thinking about the wider senses, is to doom ourselves to failure.

These various 'storeys' of the building will not necessarily follow each other in chronological order: the analogy should not be pushed so far. For most Christians the various levels will need returning to again and again: holiness of life, relationships with other believers, active submission to God's will, and the particular tasks God has for each of us. All of these are vital and none can be omitted. The building analogy points both to the logical dependence of each level on the ones below it, and also to the vital need for the lower level questions to be addressed as prerequisites of addressing the higher level issues.

That is why we shall now turn to think about each of the levels of the building in turn, starting with the foundations and working up through the floors until we reach the narrow sense of 'call'.

For Reflection

Read Psalm 19. Jot down the variety of ways in which God reveals himself in this Psalm. What are the ways in which you have experienced God speaking to you? Focus on one particular time when you were aware of God's call (in any of the senses we have thought about). Relive that time in your mind: it may help to tell the story to someone else. How far are you living out now what God's call to you was then? What might you need to do to bring your life more into line with that call?

3 *Called to Belong*

The call to belong to God through Jesus Christ is fundamental to the other dimensions of our calling. Without a
personal encounter with Christ we shall seek further guidance in vain. How does such a meeting come about? We
can begin to understand this by considering the first disciples of Jesus in the early chapters of Mark's Gospel.

THE FIRST DISCIPLES
After Jesus' period in the wilderness he returned to his
home area of Galilee, where his first action was to recruit
disciples. But Jesus did not put up a poster inviting anyone
who might be interested in following him: he issued an
authoritative command! He told Andrew and Simon that
he would make them fish for people; he *called* James and
John, who immediately left their nets and their father
Zebedee (1.16–20). Jesus' call drew out their response.

Later, as Jesus was gaining a reputation for spending
time with society's outcasts and 'sinners', he was challenged by the religious leaders, 'Why does he eat with tax-
collectors and sinners?' (2.16). In his brilliant reply Jesus
not only swept away the objection, but also clarified the
central purpose of his mission. Jesus compared his work
to that of a doctor. Doctors spend their time with sick
people, not those who are well. To go into a hospital and
find it full of people leaping about, bursting with good
health, would be crazy, because hospitals are for those
who are ill. Since Jesus' ministry was to find sinners and
lead them to be righteous – to *call . . .* sinners' – the place
where he was to be found was with the sinners. To be

anywhere else would be as strange as a doctor never seeing anyone who was ill.

People did not have to be good enough before they could follow Jesus: the reason he came was because they were not, and could never be, good enough for God. Jesus called people to follow him who knew that things were wrong between them and God. Those who thought things were all hunky-dory would be too deaf to hear the call of Jesus anyway.

Later, Jesus hand-picked a group of twelve from the wider group who went around with him, people he was going to put his time into, whom he was going to teach, whom he would send out as his representatives, and who would ultimately form the foundation of his church.[1] Mark writes that Jesus *called* them to himself. Jesus took the initiative, as he had done in calling Simon and Andrew, James and John, and as he had done in seeking out the hated tax-collectors and the sinners. He made the first move: the apostles responded to his call.

THE EARLY CHURCH

If we look at the earliest days of the church, the same pattern emerges. When Peter preaches on the day of Pentecost, he tells the listening crowd that God's promise of forgiveness and the gift of the Holy Spirit is not just for them and their children, but for *everyone* whom God calls to himself.[2] This is the same theme, of God making the first move, as we saw in the ministry of Jesus; indeed, this idea runs like a scarlet thread through the whole Bible, right from God calling to Adam and Eve when they were hiding from him[3] through to the risen and ascended Christ addressing John in the book of Revelation.[4] God's initiative is a strong theme in the whole book of Acts, seen, for example, in the story of God leading Peter to go to the Gentile Cornelius to tell him about Christ, something that Peter would not otherwise have done.[5]

This theme is particularly strong in Paul's letters, as we have already seen in Romans (in chapter 2 above). It is typical for Paul to describe Christians as those whom God has called.[6] The means that God uses to call people is the message of the gospel about his Son Jesus Christ: '[God] called you through our proclamation of the good news', Paul told the Thessalonian Christians.[7]

RESPONDING TO GOD'S CALL: BAPTISM

A very important way of responding to God's call is Christian baptism, and it is significant that the language of calling is used in the New Testament in connection with baptism. Baptism is a powerful picture of the way that a person hears Christ's invitation into a relationship and responds. Two passages particularly describe this process.

Timothy is reminded of 'the eternal life, to which you were called and for which you made the good confession in the presence of many witnesses'.[8] The most probable meaning of this verse is that Paul is reminding Timothy of his baptism, which was not only the time when he made 'the good confession' of his faith in Christ, but also the time of his response to the call to eternal life mentioned earlier in the verse.

Likewise, James speaks of unbelievers 'who blaspheme the honoured name which was called down upon you' (2.7: my translation). This is likely to be a reference to baptism because Christian baptism was baptism into the name of Jesus;[9] 'the honoured name that was called down upon you' was the name of Jesus, and the time at which it happened was the person's baptism into Christ. In other words, 'call down' is here being used of the prayer of the person doing the baptizing, who prays that Christ will come into the candidate's life. Jesus Christ is being invited into the person's life in their baptism.

In baptisms in Anglican churches, hearing and responding to Christ's call is symbolized by the questions and responses that a candidate must make:[10]

Do you believe and trust in God the Father, who made the world?
I believe and trust in him.
Do you believe and trust in his Son Jesus Christ, who redeemed mankind?
I believe and trust in him.
Do you believe and trust in his Holy Spirit, who gives life to the people of God?
I believe and trust in him.

In each case, the question presents the candidates with what God has done and they respond by stating their own belief and trust in the God who has revealed himself in that particular way, whether as Father, Son, or Holy Spirit. God's action comes first and the candidates respond to what God has done: it is the same principle of God taking the initiative that we have seen throughout our study so far.[11]

Exactly how does someone respond to God's initiative and accept what Christ offers? Consider what follows, for you yourself may be aware of wanting to respond to God's invitation for the first time, or you may want to be able to explain to someone else how to respond.

The Anglican baptism service explains the different steps of our response in the other three questions that the candidate must answer:

> Do you turn to Christ?
> *I turn to Christ.*
> Do you repent of your sins?
> *I repent of my sins.*
> Do you renounce evil?
> *I renounce evil.*

The steps involved include turning away from our past way of living, when we lived independently of God: this is the meaning of repentance. We admit that we have lived wrongly and commit ourselves not to continue in that way of life: this is what renouncing evil entails. The third step is consciously to open our lives to Christ, to turn positively towards him, to invite him to come and live within our lives. This is how we respond to God's call to come to new life, his call to us to live.

It is this third step which distinguishes Christian faith from simply turning over a new leaf and trying to be better, for it is Christ alone who can enable us to turn from our old ways and it is Christ alone who can give us the power to live differently by the gift of his Spirit.

The way to take these steps is to talk to God and say to him, first, that you recognize that you have lived with yourself at the centre of your life and not him; second, that you wish to turn away from your old way of living and never to go back; third, that you want now to live for Christ and will seek to put him and his desires first in your life; and finally, that you want Christ to give you his Holy Spirit to give you the power to live for him.

People find it helpful to talk this step over with a friend who is a Christian, perhaps before taking it or certainly afterwards. If this is a step you take, do find someone you can tell that you have done it, so that they can help you in your first days of following Christ. (There are some suggestions for helpful reading on getting started in the Christian life in the resources section at the end of this book.)

THE GOD WHO CALLS

Behind the idea of God calling people is a key theme of the Bible: the God of the Bible is a *communicator*, a God who speaks. He is not a silent idol, with a mouth but unable to utter a word; he has *no* mouth, but he *speaks* (Psalm 115.5). So the Psalmist mocks the gods of the other nations which are idols made from silver and gold, wood and stone, for the God of Israel is not impotent like them.

A distinctive mark of Christianity among the religions of the world is this belief that God has spoken in a variety of ways to call humankind to himself. He has not left us to grope about in the dark, but has given us clear directions as to the right way to go. He has not spoken merely to provide entertainment for the human race, but because he seeks a response of personal relationship with the people he has created.

Suppose I were lost on a mountain in a blizzard and could not see anything but the snow coming down. If I then heard a voice below me saying, 'Take five steps to your right and then you will be on a good path that takes you down the mountain to safety', I would not act at once: after all, I might be standing on the edge of a huge drop! First of all, I would want to find out quickly as much as possible about the voice I could hear, in order to decide whether I could trust what it said. I might ask the voice about other things in that mountain area that I knew, to see if it was a reliable guide. But the moment would come when I would need to decide whether to trust the voice and take five steps to my right to find the path.

The process by which many people hear and respond to God's call is similar to this. They may find themselves in some need or painful situation and be wondering what to do when God speaks to them. He may speak in a variety of ways, depending on the circumstances.

John McCarthy describes a time when he was in despair while he was held hostage in Lebanon and called out, 'Help me please, oh God, help me.' At once he found himself surrounded by a warm, bright light and danced, full of joy. This experience gave him new strength to carry on and a strong sense of hope that he would survive.[12] It certainly seems that God responded and visited him in his despair.

A friend of mine, who had been thinking seriously about Christian faith for some time, woke early one morning and distinctly heard his name spoken three times. For another friend it was through reading a copy of John's Gospel that she felt addressed by God. For another, it was reading

Corrie ten Boom's *The Hiding Place*, which describes how she lived out her remarkable Christian faith by hiding Jews in Holland during World War II and was finally sent to the Ravensbruck concentration camp. For me, the death of my father forced me to face ultimate questions of life and death.

God speaks in many ways to call people into a relationship with him, and Christians need to be alert to the ways in which God does this, so that we can explain to people what is going on and help them to respond appropriately.

The God of the Bible, further, is *purposeful* in his communication. He speaks to call us into a relationship with him, but he does not then stop speaking. Rather, he continues to speak to us to lead us to be more and more the people he intends us to be. He has an aim, an end in view, which is to restore the image of himself in us that has been damaged. (We shall think more about this in the next chapter.)

The God of the Bible is also *merciful and forgiving*. Some Christians speak as though to miss what God intends at one stage of your life means that he writes you off forever. Such people present a picture of the Christian life as a road where if you take one wrong turning you can never get back onto the main road. Sometimes they speak of being stuck with God's 'second best' for their lives.

None of these attitudes reflect the purposes of God in the Bible. When Christians fail, God does not give up on them, but works to restore them to a full relationship with him by leading them to turn away from their failure, to admit to him that they were wrong, and to ask his forgiveness. David is a good example of this principle at work at a number of points in his life, such as his prayer of repentance after he had sex with another man's wife, Bathsheba, and then arranged for the man, Uriah, to be killed (Psalm 51: the story is in 2 Samuel 11–12). God continued to do good things for David and allowed him to continue as king. Naturally, there were events set in train by David's sin that proved damaging later, but God did not write David off for his failure – and a very public failure, at that. When David acknowledged his wrongdoing and turned back to God, God was willing to restore David's broken relationship with him again.

CARRYING A CALL TO COMPLETION

A very encouraging use of 'call' words in the New Testament comes in the context of God completing the work he has begun in calling people to know him. Hebrews speaks of the powerful work that Jesus did in bringing the new covenant of forgiveness into being 'so that those who are called may receive the promised eternal inheritance'.[13] Likewise the angel who is John's guide tells him, 'Blessed are those who are called to the marriage-supper of the Lamb.'[14]

This highlights another key truth about God in the Bible: he will carry his call through to completion in the new heaven and the new earth. Those who respond to his call can rest secure in the confidence that God will transform them to be like his Son Jesus Christ, perfect in every way. Paul does not therefore envisage sitting back, just waiting for God to do it all. Rather, 'I press on toward the goal for the prize of the heavenly call of God in Christ Jesus.'[15] Paul saw himself as working still harder, because he knew he was answerable to Christ for the way he had lived. He did not need to work hard in order to be accepted by God, for Christ had done all that was necessary for Paul's forgiveness and adoption as a child of God. But he did not want to be ashamed when he met Christ face to face, and so he strove to serve Christ as fully as he was able.

HEARING AND RESPONDING TO GOD'S CALL TO BELONG

How can we hear and respond to God's call today, or develop and grow in our experience of God's call? We will think about two ways in which we can do this, and each entails steps that could be taken to develop a listening ear and an answering voice.

Using the Bible

The Bible has central place in hearing God's voice, for it is there that we can read the authoritative record and explanation of God's actions in the world.

Identifying with people

One method of reading the Bible, which many people find helpful, is to get inside the characters of the Bible, to try to sit where they sat and see things from their perspective. Try this for one of the characters from the Gospels below. In each case there are references to the main passages about their call to follow Jesus and how that call developed.

> *Thomas:* Mark 3.13–19 (esp. v. 18); John 11.11–16; 14.1–7; 20.24–29
>
> *Mary Magdalene:* Luke 8.2; Matthew 27.57–61; 28.1–10; Luke 24.1–11; John 20.1–2, 10–18
>
> *Mary of Bethany:* Luke 10.38–42; John 12.1–8; 11.1–46
>
> *James:* Matthew 4.21–22; Mark 5.22–24, 35–43; Matthew 10.1–2, 5–42; Mark 10.35–45; Matthew 17.1–9

A good way to do this is to find a time to be quiet to think for a while, say for fifteen minutes or so. Read through the passages for the character you have chosen and think about the person. What was life like for them before the call to follow Jesus? How did they feel? What did they do? How did their call come? What were their reactions and feelings when the call came? How did their call develop? What were their feelings then? What were the areas of growth and development as this person followed

Jesus? With imagination *become* the character, in order to get inside their skin.

If possible, talk this exercise through with someone else – or, even better, get them to choose a different character and help each other to learn from the characters each one has chosen. (If that is not possible, try writing the story down, and then think about the further questions in the light of that.) Tell them what it was like to be the character by telling your story in the first person: 'I felt . . .', 'I thought . . .', and so on. Then give them the opportunity to ask questions, still identifying with the person in the Bible, to draw out your thoughts further.

After a few minutes, step out of the character and become yourself again. Why did you choose that character? What connections did you notice between your call and response to God and the character's? Are there steps you need to take in your response to God's call in the light of those links?

Being and doing

There is a strong temptation in today's Western society, which places a high value on money and possessions, to believe that we must be active to be worthwhile as people. This is one factor in the devastation that people experience when they are made 'redundant'; even the word itself tells them that society no longer values them! It is also a factor in the low value that society apparently places on retired people or home-makers, for they are not economically productive.

The 1970s in Britain were described as the 'me decade' and this was arguably even more true of the 1980s, with the economic boom of the mid-eighties producing greater prosperity for some. Today, the power of advertising to create envy and covetousness has never been greater, and this tempts people of all ages – although the young are particularly vulnerable – to spend more than they have, to step onto the escalator of desire, always wanting more.

In such a context the tendency is for Christian people simply to mirror the state of society. We can see that tendency in the development of 'Christian' advertising which is encouraging precisely the same covetousness as its so-called 'secular' counterpart. The only difference is the language used: 'This book is indispensable to your Christian growth' (really?); 'A conference you must not miss' (why?); and so on.

In this situation the human tendency to self-justification before God is exacerbated. Our natural inclination is to believe that we are fine, that God will accept us in the end because we are really OK. This is the working belief system of most Westerners, although it is hardly a new one. In different periods Christian leaders such as Paul, Augustine of Hippo, Martin Luther and Karl Barth have rightly opposed the belief that we can be accepted by God through our achievements.

The way some churches function can encourage this belief. Newcomers, seeing the activities of a lively church, can easily gain the impression that it is by what we do *for* God that we are accepted *by* God – an impression that the members and leaders of the church may not intend to give. The services of such a church can be a hive of activity, with different people appearing at the front of church to read the Scriptures, lead in prayer, give the notices or help administer communion. They may run like clockwork, with nothing ever out of place. The model of Christian living that the church is communicating may well be heard as being that we are accepted by God because of our deeds, whatever may be said from the pulpit about God's acceptance depending only on what Christ did for us on the cross. What such a church *does* speaks louder than what it *says*. It is so easy to become the kind of church which in theory believes that we are welcomed by God through Christ alone, but acts in ways which deny it.

What kind of church life would reflect the belief that we truly are accepted by God's grace, his free love to us given in Jesus? The communion service, the eucharist, pictures this very powerfully. When we take the bread and wine we come with empty hands to receive the tokens of Christ's love for us. As we hold out our empty hand for the bread we are showing that God receives us only because of what he gives to us, the broken body of Christ symbolized in the broken bread. Our only contribution to being received by God is the sins from which we need to be delivered.

Becoming a Christian is about what God does for us through Christ, not what we do for him. Nothing we do can ever win God's welcome: we simply need to receive what he has done for us, to respond to his call. Baptism also pictures this, for we are baptized by someone else; we do not baptize ourselves. Infant baptism speaks particularly powerfully of our acceptance not being the result of our deeds, for what can an infant have done in order to be accepted by God?

Church life that reflects the belief that God accepts us on the grounds of his love for us alone will have space for God built into it. It will regularly acknowledge our dependence upon God in its prayers, hymns and songs. It will cope with mistakes happening in services, without panic that the world will end (while also seeking to reduce the number of such mistakes). It will seek to give people the space and time to listen to what God has to say to them through Scripture without pressurizing them to get involved in so much activity that there is no time or energy to be still and know that the Lord is God.

Prayer

Christian prayer is conversation with God. At times the focus may be on listening to him, at other times the focus may be on talking to him: but both elements are important.

Lawrence and Diana Osborn draw attention to the importance of the personalities of the partners in a conversation for the way that the conversation is conducted.[16] We would never dream of speaking to all the people we meet in the same way, because their personalities are different; we adapt the way we communicate to those we encounter. Traditionally, teaching on Christian prayer has focused on one partner in the conversation, God himself, without ever considering our end of the conversation. It is of course right that we should get to know more of the personality of God, in order that we may understand him better and communicate with him more effectively. But it is also important that we reflect on the personality that each of us has, and the impact that personality has on the way we speak and listen to God.

Consider the corporate prayer life of a church. It only requires a moment's thought to realize that there will be parts of that prayer life which some within the congregation find most helpful in conversing with God – and that these parts will be exactly the same ones that others find least helpful. And the reverse will often be true as well! As a result, groups can form within a congregation, each preferring different styles of prayer (often focused on the types of music used or the person leading the prayers or music). Worse, the various groups can then write one another off as unspiritual because the others do not find the same styles of prayer helpful.

The insight that our personalities are an important part of our human conversations can be transferred to our conversations with God. One valuable modern tool in helping to understand our personalities better is the Myers-Briggs Type Indicator (MBTI). This provides a measure for some aspects of human personality which can then be applied to understand the approaches to prayer (and to many other things too) that different personality types will find most helpful and accessible.

Briefly, the MBTI works by considering four pairs of polar opposites in human personality. The assumption is that, while each of us can and does use both sides, we each have a preference for one of each pair, rather like each of us being naturally right- or left-handed. No value judgement is implied by these preferences: all of them have their own strengths and weaknesses. The personality type that we have is then described by the combination of the four preferences.

The first pair is *Extraversion (E)/Intraversion (I)* (terms which do not mean in MBTI what they are commonly understood to mean). This is to do with whether our preference is to spend time in the outer world of objects and people or the inner world of ideas and feelings. Extraverts tend to be activists; intraverts tend to be more reflective.

The second pair is *Sensing (S)/Intuition (N)*. This is to do with how we gather information about the external world, whether by collecting data from our senses (S) or looking for patterns, for the 'big picture' (N: this is different from the common idea of intuition as non-rational jumps in thinking). Sensers enjoy colour, music and are more present-oriented, whereas intuitives are more future-oriented, looking at the possibilities conjured up by the present.

The third pair is *Thinking (T)/Feeling (F)*, and centres on how we make our decisions. A thinker will work things through step by step, whereas a feeler tends to 'just know' what to do. Thinkers use logic, cause and effect, and other objective criteria to make their decisions; feelers use personal, ethical, or aesthetic criteria.

The fourth pair is *Perceiving (P)/Judging (J)*. This is to do with our basic orientation on life, whether we habitually make decisions about the external world and therefore organize and control it (J: this is different from being judgemental) or prefer to 'go with the flow' of what is happening (P). Perceivers love new experiences and often act spontaneously, whereas judgers like things to be planned ahead.

The result of a Myers-Briggs analysis (done by completing a questionnaire) is a set of four letters which sum up the preferences a person has in each of these pairs, such as INTJ. This combination means that the person described gains energy and inspiration from the internal world of ideas rather than the external world of people and objects; collects information intuitively, seeing the big picture and the patterns in it rather than having such an eye for detail; makes decisions by reasoning them out logically; and prefers to handle the external world by organizing and controlling it, rather than simply going along with whatever comes.

This kind of analysis can be very helpful in understanding a number of things about ourselves. In a Christian context it can assist in identifying the ways in which we find it most helpful to pray, both individually and with other Christians. It also throws up the interesting question as to how far the services in a church offer each of the personality types elements that they will find helpful in speaking and listening to God. It is all too easy for a church to adopt the preferences of one personality type, or group of types, to the exclusion of others.

As examples of different types of prayer that different types latch on to, consider the following. A senser may find praying aloud comes more naturally to them, whereas an intuitive may find symbols or pictures help them to respond to God more. Likewise, a feeler may find lively, charismatic-style worship particularly helpful, whereas a thinker may prefer listening to a well structured Bible exposition. Remember that each of these pairs of polar opposites is not exclusive: all of us have some ability at both poles of each pair. It is important not to ignore the poles that do not come naturally to us (our 'shadow', as it is often called in MBTI analysis) in order to develop as fully rounded people. But we do have preferences and it is wise to be aware what they are. (There are suggestions for further reading and action on MBTI in the resources list at the end of this book.)

A call to share

Responding to God's call to belong to him ourselves means that we will want to help others to hear the voice of Christ calling them too to faith in him. To belong to Christ carries with it the responsibility to 'be ready to give a reason for the hope that you have' (1 Peter 3.15, my translation). One of the surest ways to grow in our own knowledge of God is to share that knowledge with others.

This is the responsibility and privilege of all who belong to Jesus Christ, not just of a select few, whether clergy or missionaries or other seemingly 'special' people. The New Testament is clear that, while God gives *some* Christians a particular gift as evangelists, *all* Christians are to be witnesses to Christ. The distinction is that evangelists are those whom God regularly uses to lead others to faith in Christ, whereas witnesses are people who speak of what they have personally experienced when called upon to do so.

God uses his people to call new people to belong to him through Jesus, and nothing will help Christians to get to know God better than to begin to take the risks involved in speaking of Jesus Christ to those who do not yet know him. Answering their questions and helping them to see why faith is reasonable will make Christians think issues out in a way that little else will. Further, research shows that it is through personal contact with a Christian that the vast majority of people come to faith, so we should seek opportunities to commend Christ to others.

This is an important theme for Graham, the local councillor mentioned at the start of this book, to consider. Part of the reason that he is reaching a point of crisis over his political involvement is the fact that he virtually never speaks openly about his Christian faith among his political colleagues. Hardly any of them know that he goes to church and he feels embarrassed about mentioning the fact, even though he sees his faith as a mainspring of his political commitments. This makes it extremely difficult for him to voice the problems he faces with party policy. Graham needs to pray for opportunities to speak openly with his party colleagues about his faith in Christ in ways that will make it easier to then explain his reservations about policies; he needs to ask the members of his church house group to pray for that, as well as for great wisdom in his work as a local councillor.

CALLED TO BELONG

The call to belong to Jesus Christ is a thrilling call, as God calls us from the death of our sinfulness to new life. It is a call to which we need to respond gladly, and a call we need to share with others.

But things do not stop there! When we come to belong to Christ we begin a lifetime of progress and growth in our relationship with him. That is the second level of 'call' as the New Testament writers understand it, and we shall think about that in the next chapter.

For Reflection

Read slowly and thoughtfully Ephesians 2.1–10. Note down the state we were in before God called us to belong to him through Christ, and the state we are now in. Spend some time giving thanks to God for what he has done for you personally in this way.

From among your family, friends and acquaintances, choose two or three who are not yet Christians and begin to pray for them regularly. Pray that you may speak to them about faith in Christ and that God will, in time, bring them to know and love him too.

4 *Called to Be*

We noticed earlier (chapter 2) that the important phrase in Romans 1.7 and 1 Corinthians 1.2 can be understood in two ways: as 'called to be *saints*' or 'called to be *holy*'. Both dimensions – our distinctive, holy lifestyle and our relationships with other Christians – are important elements in the New Testament's understanding of the Christian calling.

It is not that God's call to these things is separate from the call to belong to Jesus Christ: it is more an unpacking of that first call. In the New Testament letters the Christian life is often described using the image of a *walk*; it is an image that would have come from the writers' Jewish background, since the rabbis spoke of teaching about lifestyle as 'how to walk' (*halakah*). Three examples, two from Paul and one from Peter, show the intimate link between Christian lifestyle and the call to belong to God through Christ.

Paul speaks of 'walking worthily of the calling with which you were called [by God]',[1] implying that the Christian life is a response to God's initiative in calling us to belong to him. God's call is like a seed that is planted, which contains within itself the material that will produce the full flower in due time, given the right conditions. It is not that God calls us and then leaves us to our own devices, but rather that the original call has within it what is necessary for the end product, our final perfection when we see Christ face to face.

Paul also writes, 'We exhorted you and encouraged and testified that you should walk worthily of the God who calls you into his own kingdom and glory.'[2] Here Paul reminds the Thessalonian Christians that their lifestyle is to be modelled on the character of the God who called them; indeed, Paul sees God's calling not just as a past event, but as a continuing activity, so he uses the present tense: God 'calls' them to this way of living. Believers are being called to reflect the character of the God who first called them to faith in him and who continues that call day by day in the nitty-gritty of Christian living.

Peter later describes this process in another way when he exhorts his readers to 'be all the more eager to confirm your call and election'.[3] Their lives must show the fruit of God's call in such characteristics as goodness, knowledge, self-control, endurance, godliness, mutual affection and love,[4] which, interestingly, includes in the one theme the two dimensions that we have seen in Paul, of distinctive, holy lifestyle and relationships with fellow Christians. Peter teaches that, though good living cannot save them from their sins, they will not ultimately be saved without their faith in God being displayed in the way that they live. The life of obedience is evidence that their claim to have responded to God's call to belong to Christ really is genuine. And Peter is clear that this living out of God's call is only possible with God's strength: '[Jesus'] divine power has given us everything needed for life and godliness.'[5]

These passages in the letters make it clear, in different ways, that the dual call to holy living and Christian relationships is all of a piece with the call to come into the Christian community in the first place. Let's now think in more detail about how the two dimensions are to be worked out.

CALLED TO HOLINESS

The call to holiness is not a call to dullness! Holiness, rightly understood, is human life as it is meant to be lived. Being holy is being fully human, for we are created in God's image and likeness and meant to reflect in our lives the nature and character of our creator God. Just as God is a holy God, perfect, pure, consistent, just, and merciful, so his people are to be like him: 'as he who called you is holy, be holy yourselves in all your conduct.'[6]

Being distinctive in this way is not easy, for it can involve swimming against the tide, something that is never straightforward. John Dean was one of the Watergate conspirators and worked very closely with Richard Nixon. He said that the situation in the White House during the Nixon administration was 'to get along you have to go along'. If you wanted to get along, to progress in the political scene of that time, you had to go along, to suppress your scruples and values, at least sometimes. The breaking of the Watergate scandal showed just how far human beings could be corrupted when the enticements of power were dangled before them.

By contrast, consider the Old Testament character Joseph in Egypt. When he was first there, Joseph found himself promoted in his master Potiphar's household to a position of great responsibility and trust: everything that Potiphar had was given into Joseph's charge, and Potiphar was a powerful and wealthy man. At that point Potiphar's wife noticed how handsome and attractive Joseph was, and invited Joseph to have sex with her. In refusing her invitation Joseph explained that he could not do such a thing, not just because it would be betraying his master's trust, nor because it would be extremely dangerous if they were found out, but because to do it would be to 'sin against God'.[7] Joseph had what are sometimes called 'counter-values' to sustain him against the temptation presented by Potiphar's wife. It was the knowledge that he lived in the presence of God and under the rule of God that held him back. And for Joseph, this was a costly choice, for the result was that he was thrown into jail when his master's wife then falsely accused him of having attempted to rape her.

Joseph provides a model of this distinctive lifestyle to which Christians are called, especially in his motivation, for it is the knowledge that we live under the eye of God that will guard us against giving in and going along with the tide. It is that knowledge that will sustain us when doing the right thing (or avoiding the wrong thing) is costly.

This same theme is reflected in the use of the two words 'lead' and 'guide' in the Bible. Again and again they are used of God leading his people into paths of righteousness, of right living.[8] Virtually never are these words used of specific choices about whether to take up a particular occupation, or marry a certain person, or go to live in a certain place – all the things that Christians commonly think of when they speak of 'guidance'. Scripture is centrally concerned with God's guidance for living, which is focused much more on the kind of people we are than on such specific choices. Where we live, whether we marry (and who) and what our occupation is to be, are all secondary as far as God's purposes are concerned. His principal aim is to see us grow in holiness, a process he will bring to completion at the last day.

Further, holiness is an important prerequisite to seeking guidance over these kinds of 'vocational choices'. The Psalmist describes his experience of answered prayer in writing, 'If I had cherished iniquity in my heart, the Lord would not have listened. But truly God has listened; he has given heed to the words of my prayer.'[9] I first met this verse in my early days as a Christian as an explanation of why prayer sometimes seems unanswered: if we are in deliberate sin and rebellion against God in some area of our life, then God stops listening to our prayers until we put that area right. We do this by admitting our disobedience honestly to God and asking his forgiveness, turning away from the wrong we have done and resolving not to fail in that way again, and, if another person is involved, putting things right with them too.

The Psalm is here describing a situation where we *know* that we are disobeying God and we are refusing to put it right, not the situation that we are all in, that we are disobeying God at some point in our life. It is not that God does not listen to us if there is *any* wrong in our lives, for then he would never listen at all. Rather, it is deliberate, conscious rebellion against him that turns God deaf, since the first thing that needs to happen in that situation is for our relationship with him to be opened up again. For communication to flow, the blockage of our sin needs removing.

Holiness is a whole-life quality, not just an in-church quality. Peter tells his readers to 'be holy . . . in *all* your conduct'. Christians in the past – and still today – have sometimes thought of holiness as a quality of otherworldliness, separate from daily life. At the time of the Reformation in Holland, as a mark of the call of God affecting the whole of life, Reformed Christians locked their church doors on Sunday nights. People had previously felt that the church was the house of God, to which you came to worship, to pray, to light your candle: that building was the place where you met God. The Dutch Reformers took a different view: they believed that God was there to be met and served in every part of life, not just when Christians met together on Sunday, and as a symbol of that they locked their church doors, to show that Christ's rule was over the whole of life and not confined to the church building.[10]

CALLED TO A CORPORATE LIFE

Paul's description, 'called to be *saints*', means that Christian people, because they are called to belong to Jesus Christ, are also called to belong to each other. For the New Testament writers, the Christian life is by nature a corporate enterprise: we have been 'called into the fellowship of his Son, Jesus Christ our Lord'.[11]

Further, many of the key qualities of Christian living – forbearance, patience, gentleness, forgiveness and many more – need other people in order for them to be practised. A glance at Colossians 3 (for example) shows that it cannot be taken for granted that Christians will treat each other rightly, for Paul has to urge his readers to 'put to death . . . whatever in you is earthly' (v. 5), listing such things as fornication, impurity, passion, evil desire, greed, anger, wrath, malice, slander, abusive language, and lies. No one reading this catalogue of vices could believe that the earliest Christians were always loving, patient, and kind towards one another!

The corporate dimension of the Christian life is not easy to practise at any time or in any age, for human beings are fallible and sinful, but our age and culture may be one where it is harder than in many others. Modern Westerners have been encouraged to see themselves as autonomous, free-standing individuals by 200 years of thought and life since the movement known as the Enlightenment. This was a complex movement of ideas in Europe and America, but a central belief held by many thinkers of that time was that human reason is the key to unlock the universe. Enlightenment thinking provided a basis for much modern science and technology to develop, but it could also be deeply hostile to religion. It was the abandonment of a real sense of dependence on God by some Enlightenment thinkers that led to human beings being seen as alone in the universe, having to choose their own destiny and not needing the crutch of religion. (This was by contrast with the acknowledgement of God which had been the hallmark of early Christian scientific thinkers such as Isaac Newton.)

As late twentieth-century people we inherit the results of two centuries of thinking along these lines, for example, in the stress in some political thought on providing more and more 'freedom' for the individual without a balancing concern for the needs of others. 'There is no such thing as society' may or may not be taken out of context as an expression of Margaret Thatcher's thinking, but it certainly summarizes the results of this current of thought. Such thinking grew stronger through the sixties, the decade of individual choice and liberty, and the seventies, the 'me decade', to produce the political climate of the eighties in Britain and elsewhere, where the dismantling of state control was the watchword of successive governments.

In such a climate there is a strong temptation for Christians to be sucked into the world's way of thinking. This results in Christians whose sole stress is on 'my relationship with God'. In the sphere of evangelism, such people speak of individual witness, but shy away from corporate Christian witness against evils in society.

Following the world's way of thinking results in a consumerist approach to church membership, where the church we join is chosen on the basis of what we will receive from belonging to it, rather than the opportunities for giving to others in and through the life of that church. If the church we belong to does not provide what we want, we will move somewhere that will do so. The burgeoning of denominations and the huge growth of independent churches can be read, at one level, as the result of church members adopting a 'consumer' approach to churchgoing. (It can, of course, be seen on the other hand as the result of sterility and the refusal to change on the part of the leadership of some of the traditional churches which could be the result of another form of individualism, but this time adopted by those leaders.)

The corporate dimension of the Christian life is a vital factor in seeking and knowing more of what God's call for us should be, both individually and as fellowships of Christians. As we have noted, the whole discussion of Colossians 3 is concerned with Christian relationships. The (very common) view of v. 15, 'the peace that Christ gives is to guide you in the decisions that you make' (*Good News Bible*), is that it refers to *inner* peace, to peaceful feelings. Some Christians make their decisions because they feel this 'sense of peace' about a particular course of action. But the whole context of the chapter, let alone the second half of v. 15, shows that this is mistaken.

Two points need to be grasped about this passage to see how vital it is for Christian decision-making. First, the 'heart' in Scripture does not refer to the seat of the feelings and emotions, but to the will and the mind. This means that experiencing peace in our hearts is more to do with allowing Christ's rule to affect our judgement and treatment of other Christians, as the second half of the verse makes clear, 'to which [peace] you were called in the one body'. Tom Wright comments:

> . . . whatever disagreements or mutual suspicions occur in the church, they are to be dealt with at the deepest level, by all parties allowing the fact of their unity in Christ to settle the issue in their hearts. The *pax Christiana* is to prevail in the church, as the *pax Romana* did in the world of Paul's day, allowing its inhabitants to pursue their respective callings without the constant threat of war.[12]

The views and comments of other Christians will therefore be highly significant in our decision-making. This was the case in Paul's own life at several points, such as when Barnabas was willing to stick his neck out and introduce Paul (then known by his Jewish name of Saul) to the highly suspicious Christian leaders in Jerusalem,[13] or when he later chose Paul to help him in teaching the new church at Antioch.[14] Indeed, Paul's call to his main life's-work, of evangelism among non-Jewish people, was both confirmed and taken forward with the support of the church at Antioch, for it was through them that God spoke to initiate the new move.[15]

Second, 'the peace of Christ' is simply not a feeling in the New Testament, but an objective description of what we experience because of Christ's death for us. The peace *of* God is peace *with* God, the state of being reconciled to God, forgiven and accepted. Thus it is the fact that Christ has accepted each of us that is to be decisive for Christian relationships. This fact is to guard us against social one-upmanship in the church, for whatever reason, and it is to result in mutual acceptance and welcome, for Christ has welcomed each of us.[16]

Again, the result of understanding this is that we shall take the advice and wisdom of our sisters and brothers in Christ extremely seriously. It was the church at large that chose the seven who were given the tricky job of handling the church's care for its more needy members.[17] The apostles sought the whole church's advice rather than, on the one hand, making an autocratic decision on their own or, on the other hand, asking for volunteers.

As a modern example of these principles at work, consider the Church of England's selection of potential ministers. In the ordination service the congregation is asked by the bishop:

> Those whose duty it is to inquire about these persons and examine them have found them to be of godly life and sound learning, and believe them to be duly called to serve God in this ministry. Is it therefore your will that they should be ordained?[18]

The bishop refers here to two levels of the church's involvement in the selection process. There are 'those whose duty it is to inquire', which includes the diocesan staff who see potential candidates, the selectors at a selection conference, the bishop who makes a decision on the basis of the selectors' advice, and the staff of the candidate's theological college or course. There is also the congregation present at the ordination, usually including members of the churches where those being ordained will serve. Both groups are asked whether they support the ordination of the candidate, indicating that a call to ordination is not a private matter between the individual and God, but must involve the church.

PURSUING HOLINESS IN A CORPORATE CONTEXT

Bringing these two dimensions together, what does it mean to pursue holiness as a body of Christians? The key will be working out in practice the belief that God really has called us to be members of one body. That involves learning 'dignified dependence' on other Christians.

'Dignified dependence' is a phrase that is used in caring for older people, and signifies a style of care that provides people with what they need, while at the same time ensuring that their human worth and dignity are preserved. This means involving such people in decisions about their care and lifestyle, rather than making decisions for them. Such caring provides resources for them to do as much as possible for themselves, rather than disabling them by doing too much for them.

In a Christian context the idea of dignified dependence will produce a culture within churches which combines recognition of the importance of each member's own relationship with God with the need for mutual support and encouragement to allow that relationship with God to reach its full potential.

Christian encouragement and hope is more than 'the power of positive thinking', for it is based on Christ's actions in securing a solid hope for us through his death – a death in which he stood in the place of hopelessness in bearing the consequences of our rebellion against God.

My observation is that, in general, women are rather better at offering such encouragement than men. Biblical examples of relationships of mutual support and encouragement are often of two (or more) women, such as Ruth and Naomi or Mary and Martha (although there is David and Jonathan too, but that stands out precisely because it is exceptional). There seems to be something about being a woman in our society today that allows a greater sharing of feelings – both of pain and joy – than is generally acceptable for a man. For men, feelings can be shared at a sports event but in few other contexts. Women often share and collaborate more naturally with each other in this way.

Here is an area where church life has much to learn from women's ways of being and doing, moving our churches from being male-oriented to being human-oriented. The earliest Christians certainly saw sharing our lives with each other as important: 'Bear one another's burdens', 'confess your sins to one another and pray for one another', 'love one another with mutual affection; outdo one another in showing honour';[19] and many more examples could be found simply by looking up the uses of the phrase 'one another' in a Bible concordance.

Church life for dignified dependence

Three fundamental qualities are necessary for a church that wants to pursue holiness in its life together, developing real interdependence.

First, there must be *meaningful fellowship*. This is not creating something that does not already exist, for Paul's view is that Christians *are* interdependent (for good or ill), not that they *should* be: 'If one member suffers, all suffer together . . . if one member is honoured, all rejoice together.'[20] As so often in the Christian life, we need to become what, by the grace of God, we already *are*.

To see this kind of fellowship built takes real love and acceptance of one another. It has to begin with, and be modelled by, those in leadership. Leaders need to be accepting of all whom God has brought together into the local church, whether these are the kind of people they would naturally choose to associate with or not. They also need to be models in sharing their lives with others in the congregation, rather than standing aloof.

There was a style of church leadership fashionable at one time which insisted that church leaders should not have friends within the congregation they served, for to do so would create jealousy and make some feel excluded. This led to clergy who seemed distant and stand-offish, and to churches where the clergy were seen as a race apart. The great danger of such a way of working is that the church members copy what the clergy do, and ignore any exhortation or teaching that the clergy give about mutual support and sharing: they copy what they see done, not what they hear said. The New Testament teaching about mutual care and support does not exclude the clergy; they are to seek and find much of their support in the local church to which they belong.

This involves, for those in leadership, a readiness to share weaknesses with others. This is true at every level of church life, whether in house groups, children's or teenagers' groups, women's groups, or church leadership teams. If the message that the members of the group receive is that those in leadership appear to have no weaknesses – or at least, none that they will admit to – then the group members will clam up about their weaknesses.

This is not a plea for 'letting it all hang out', for leaders to dump their problems on anyone and everyone they meet. There are times and places when it is inappropriate to do that, because the focus is the other person or people. But equally, there must be times and places when it is appropriate for leaders to share their own failings and pains with others and gain support and encouragement from them.

This does not happen overnight, but takes time to build. Most often, key steps forward in fellowship and sharing will happen through pain: when one person shares an area of pain or difficulty with another. It is then that the reality of being the body of Christ becomes evident, as we share each other's pains and burdens.

Such fellowship will provide and involve real mutual encouragement to grow in our relationship with God. To illustrate this, Graham Cray tells the story of hell going bust and the devil having to sell his tools. As people walked around on the day before the sale inspecting what was on offer, they were surprised at the prices. Exquisite instruments of torture were priced very cheaply: thumbscrews at £1 a pair, a rack at £10 and so on. Then someone noticed hanging on the wall a huge, blunt, club-like instrument, priced at £1 million. They asked the devil why this was so expensive, when the other things seemed so cheap. He replied, 'Ah, that one. That's discouragement: that gets everyone.'

Nothing will hold us back more in seeking to grow in Christian faith than the feeling of discouragement, the feeling that we are getting nowhere, that we are worse than anyone else, that we are no good. Nothing will help us forward faster than real encouragement, the feeling that we are making progress and moving on, and that we are not alone. Christian leaders have a key role in actively encouraging those who take on responsibilities. We take great care to encourage children as they grow up: when a child starts to walk for the first time and falls over after one or two steps, we do not say to the child, 'Well that wasn't very good. You should have sorted out your balance and how to put one foot in front of the other before you tried that.' No. We encourage the child, we tell him or her how well they have done. Why, then, do we stop doing that when we deal with adults? We need to offer far more positive comments than negative ones to one another, especially when someone takes on a new task.

The second quality that church life will need in order to develop dignified dependence is *discernment*. The local church is to display, in Paul's vision, a range of God-given gifts that will provide for its needs. These gifts will be God's instruments in building up the church, numerically and in depth. Therefore, identifying who has which gifts is a highly significant task in the life of the church; this is the role of discernment.

Discernment means taking care when a new person is asked to try something, that they have a good chance of doing well. This will then feed into the encouragement that we have already thought about. At times discernment will involve risk-taking, in inviting someone to do something for the first time. But if such risks are taken in an environment of real love and mutual acceptance, the person invited to take on the new task will know that they will not be destructively criticized if they make mistakes or get it wrong in some way.

Third, such a church will need *teaching and pastoral care*. Good teaching will point people towards God's concerns and aims. Paul's speech to the elders of the Ephesian church[21] shows how vital Paul saw teaching to be for the life of the church, for he says that he 'did not shrink from doing anything helpful, proclaiming the message to you and teaching you publicly and from house to house'. Such teaching will certainly include the nature of the church and its members' life together, but will also provide a Christian framework for thinking and living as the people of God. That will keep a balance in the church's life between the variety of emphases in the Bible, by helping Christians to see how different truths relate to one another.

This teaching ministry will be backed up by pastoral care, as Paul's was. He says that 'for three years I did not cease day or night to warn everyone of you with tears.' The evidence suggests that 'pastor and teacher' is to be regarded as one role, rather than two distinct ones,[22] and this implies that teaching is not to be done from a position of lofty isolation, but from a place of real involvement in people's lives. This will mean that corporate teaching will have greater relevance, and that teaching can be carried through into people's lives in personal dialogue and application.

Ken and Sally's vicar, Chris, needs to pursue with them how far they really are involved with the lives of other

Christian people. As he talks with them about their idea that God might be calling them to overseas missionary service, he will want to ask about the views of other Christians who know them well – in fact, it is because of other people's suggestions that Ken and Sally have got to the point of talking to Chris at all. He will also want to ensure that Ken is not running away from serving Christ in a tough situation in the financial field, given that the need for Christian people there is just as great as the need for those in missionary work overseas. There is also the important question of whether the skills and gifts they have to offer would be useful in an overseas setting, and a few letters or 'phone calls to missionary societies will answer that: another dimension of the input of the body of Christ into a couple's own decision-making.

For Reflection

1. Spend some time reading through Paul's description of the qualities of love in 1 Corinthians 13.4–8. Then re-read the passage and put your own name in place of 'love': 'Steve is patient, Steve is kind . . .' Think about the areas where you fail to be the holy, distinctive person God intends you to be and ask God's forgiveness and strength in those areas. Thank God for his love for us in Christ that makes our acceptance and forgiveness possible.

2. Read and think more widely about Paul's portrait of the church in 1 Corinthians. What were the faults of that church? What remedies did Paul suggest?

Are there Christians you really trust? If so, give thanks to God for them, and pray that you may be as much a support and encouragement to them as they are to you. If not, think where you might find such support and encouragement in your church, and ask God to lead you to such people. Pray for your church leaders that God will enable them to lead your church forward in ways of mutual help.

5 *Called to Let God Be God*

The God of the Bible is not passive, sitting back and waiting for human beings to take the initiative. He is active, making the first move in bringing about a relationship with us. He is active, providing what is needed for us to live in a continuing, growing relationship with him – not least through the support, encouragement, challenge, and stimulus of our fellow believers. And God's initiative and activity do not stop there, for he is committed to carrying his purposes for our lives through to completion, when we see him face to face (see chapter 2). It is this last dimension of calling, that God's calling accomplishes things, that we are going to get to grips with next.

THE GIVING OF NAMES
About a third of the uses of 'call' in the New Testament are for naming, such as 'Simon, who was called Peter'.[1] Names could be very significant in biblical times, much more so than today. In modern times we regard a name as merely a label for someone, to distinguish that person from others. We do not generally choose a name because it says something important about the child, but because it sounds good, or we like it, or we want to name the child after a relative or friend. (The exception to this, of course, is giving someone a nickname later in life, when the nickname is given just because it does reflect some characteristic of the person.)

By contrast, in biblical times the giving of names was often very significant. The name might contain a statement about the person's origins, such as Samuel, so named because he was born in answer to his mother's prayer, or Moses, so called by an Egyptian princess because she drew him out of the water.[2] The name might embody a promise or prophecy of God, such as Isaiah's son Shear-jashub, whose name means 'a remnant shall return', or Jesus himself, whose name means 'God to the rescue'.[3] Changes of name were important too, notably the change from Abram (= 'exalted father') to Abraham (= 'father of many').[4] The change of name meant that, after that time, every time anyone spoke to Abraham by name, he was reminded of God's promise that he would be the father of many.

A second side to the giving of names is that to give another a name implied a certain authority of the giver of the name over the receiver of the name. This can be seen in Adam naming the animals.[5] This is another facet to God renaming Abram as Abraham: it reflects God's authority over Abram.

God gives names

It is in this context that three 'name-giving' passages in the New Testament should be seen. John writes, 'See what love the Father has given us, that we should be called children of God; and that is what we are.'[6] John is saying that 'children of God' is not just a nice sounding, but empty, label that God attaches to people. God really does adopt us as his own sons and daughters and declares this by calling us his own children. David Jackman comments, 'Not only does he [God] give us his name . . . he gives us his status.'[7] When God says something, it really is so. His speech is powerfully effective: he has the authority to make such a declaration.

A similar idea can be seen in two places in Jesus' teaching in the Sermon on the Mount. Jesus says, 'Blessed are the peacemakers, for they will be *called* children of God' and, 'whoever breaks one of the least of these commandments, and teaches others to do the same, will be *called* least in the kingdom of heaven; but whoever does them and teaches them will be *called* great in the kingdom of heaven.'[8]

Instead of saying, 'God will call them great in the kingdom of heaven' (which is the probable meaning), Jesus uses the passive 'will be called', in line with the common Jewish practice of not using the name of God, out of reverence. Jesus' statements are God's verdict on the different sorts of people being described. Again we can see the two themes, the significance of names and the authority of the name-giver.

The authority of God is seen in his statements about the people: peacemakers will be called God's children. God himself will declare them to be his own offspring, for their character as peacemakers reflects his character as a peace-making God: like parent, like child. Likewise, those who value and revere the Old Testament Scriptures (the issue in Jesus' teaching here) will be those God declares to be great in his kingdom – God will honour them because of the way that they have honoured his written word in the Scriptures.

God's powerful word

In all three of these passages God's declaration accomplishes something. His words are not empty, but powerful and effective: he is the God 'who calls into existence the things that do not exist'.[9] Here Paul is alluding to the creation story, when God spoke the universe into being out of nothingness: six times in that story Genesis records that 'God said . . . and it was so'.[10] When God speaks, things happen: even things that do not yet exist jump to attention! Paul mentions the creation story to reinforce the point he is making about the dependability of God, who fulfilled his promise to Abraham that he would become the father of many – in spite of all the odds being against it.

These uses of 'call' combine to point to the power and trustworthiness of God. He is able to carry out his word. When he declares us to be adopted as his children, he has the authority to carry that through. It is not that he says nice things, but is unable to bring them into effect; rather, he says only what he can carry through to completion. So when God speaks and names us as his children, he is committed to completing the job: 'the gifts and the calling of God are irrevocable'.[11]

THE RESULTS OF GOD'S POWER
Three key results flow from this sense of 'call': it provides a basis for Christian confidence; it sets us free from the pressure to perform; and it assures us that wherever God sends us, he will equip and empower us.

Christian confidence
One vitally important result of God's commitment to completing his work in us is that we can be confident in his ability to bring us to perfection in heaven. We do not have to wake up every day wondering if we will be able to keep going in our Christian walk, because God has committed himself to finishing the job. He gives us his Spirit as the down payment of the great things that are to come,[12] both to reassure us that he will give us the other things in due time, and to equip and strengthen us to live for him now.

This means that Christian assurance of eternal life is not arrogance, as some suggest it is. It would indeed be arrogant to say that we are sure of eternal life if it depended on us; but it depends entirely on the gift of God to us, sealed by his Spirit dwelling in our lives. Our eternal life and our place in heaven come to us guaranteed by the promise and word of God himself – and it would be arrogant indeed to refuse to trust one who has proved himself so dependable.

The pressure to perform
The promise of eternal life that God gives to us has a further result. Because we can be confident now of our final acceptance with God, this takes off us the pressure to

succeed. The Puritan Christians of the seventeenth century understood this well. William Perkins is an example; his book *A Treatise of the Vocations* (1605) is a classic of the period. A central theme in Perkins' writing is the need for contentment with what you have and not seeking 'abundance', by which he meant excess. He recognized that some receive riches, but observed that such riches may come for a variety of reasons: because of their sin; because the devil is using riches to tempt them; or because of the blessing of God. (Perkins would not have shared the 'prosperity teaching' of some modern Western Christians, who believe that anyone who trusts God can become wealthy!)

Thus Perkins taught that Christians need not strive and struggle for success, nor constantly worry about it. Christians, because they know acceptance by God, can be content with what God gives. Their primary focus will be on faithfulness to the God who loves them and has made them his own children by adoption. So yes, they will work hard, in the knowledge that their work is 'done for the Lord'. But they will not lose sleep over things, because their acceptance ultimately depends upon what *God* has done in the life, death, and resurrection of Jesus Christ, and the gift of the Spirit, not on their success.

Someone has described the Puritans as being like people who had swallowed a gyroscope: they had *inner* bearings which kept their focus on God, their North Pole, and his direction for their lives, rather than being pulled off course by the magnetic attractions of the world, the flesh, and the devil. By contrast, some modern Christians seem more like they have swallowed a Gallup poll: their concern is focused purely on what is relevant, what modern people find acceptable and believable, without a corresponding focus on God's revelation of himself. The result is that they lack the sense of being locked in on God's concerns.

All of this provides a Christian basis for decisions about opportunities to climb the ladder of success, particularly in the world of work. For some Christians it will be right to rise to high positions, but their concern will not be with their success or otherwise, but with their own faithfulness to God. Therefore, they will resist the pressure to adopt a highly affluent lifestyle, because their central concern is God's honour and glory.

A fine example of this was Sir John Laing, the builder, who made an agreement with God when he was a young man that he would give away any excess above the basic amount of money he needed to live on. This agreement was made at a time of great crisis, when Laing's company was facing potentially crippling litigation.[13] Eventually his business prospered greatly and Laing had a very great income. But he kept his agreement with God and gave large sums of money to Christian mission work. He was also ready to share his faith with those he met (even, on one occasion, while waiting for an investiture at Buckingham Palace!), and he showed a great concern for straightforwardness and honesty in his business dealings. When Laing died in January 1978 his net estate was £371, all that was left out of the millions that had gone through his hands. He had given the rest away, and many who now love and trust Christ owe this to missionaries and Christian workers whom Laing had helped to support or train.

On the other hand, there is also the possibility that a Christian might deliberately decline promotion and advancement at work because of greater needs in other areas. For example, someone may be involved in leadership in the children's groups in their church and therefore decline a business opportunity or a promotion that would constantly take them away at weekends, because they believe that God's greatest concern for their life is their work with the children. Their sense of calling to serve God in that way will override the pressure to succeed in the business world, and will enable them to face the sacrifice of the missed opportunity. Christians should not be people the firm owns, body and soul, for it is their heavenly Father who does that.

For both sorts of Christians – those called by God to climb the ladder and those called by God to serve him in other ways – the primary concern will always be the calling of God: which is the way *he* wants them to go? This is more important than financial success, material comfort, or acceptance in the secular world. Christian contentment is a rare virtue these days, but one that needs cultivation. The same Paul who wrote, 'straining forward to what lies ahead, I press on towards the goal for the prize of the heavenly call of God in Christ Jesus,' using strenuous language of his work, also wrote, 'In any and all circumstances I have learned the secret of being well-fed and going hungry, of having plenty and being in need.'[14]

God's equipping for the task

Another result of our confidence in God's ability to complete the work that he has begun in our lives is that we can be assured that when God calls us to a task, he will always equip us to do it. He will never leave us in the lurch, struggling on our own. At times, we may be surprised by the direction in which he takes us, but he is not a cosmic sadist who delights in getting his children into situations where they will fail miserably and be utterly crushed.

That is not to say that when God calls us to perform a task for him it will be easy. Doing the right thing may at times lead to suffering and persecution, as the woman who anointed Jesus discovered.[15] But it is to say that we need to be ready for God to work through us. We can be confident that, if we want God to use us to bring honour to him, then he will do that – and he will provide us with what we need to do his will.

Gladys Aylward, a remarkable woman who served as a missionary in China from 1930 for nearly twenty years, exemplifies God's equipping of an unlikely person. Gladys was working as a parlour-maid, but was convinced that God wanted her to go to China, and so she went as a probationer to the China Inland Mission Centre in London to study. She struggled with her studies, until the Principal told her that she would have to leave the Centre and could not be a missionary in China. The assumption was that her lack of educational ability disqualified her from the task, although Gladys had been a Christian worker among young girls and prostitutes in Swansea and had preached on the streets of London.

In spite of her rejection by the Mission, Gladys went back to being a servant and saved the money to go by train to China – a highly dangerous journey at a time of war in that country – having made contact with an elderly lady, Jeannie Lawson, who longed for a younger woman to carry on her work. Gladys wrote that she believed 'that as God had worked for the men and women in the Bible so he could work for me.'[16]

The rest of her story is quite remarkable, underlining again and again the faithfulness of God in providing what she needed. Certainly, she was very determined to go and serve God in China, but that stemmed from her rock-solid conviction that God would give her what she needed to serve him there.

A contemporary example is the present Archbishop of Canterbury, George Carey, who left school without any paper qualifications to his name. When he came to faith in Christ in his later teens and began to sense that God wanted him to train to be ordained in the Church of England, he studied at night school and worked hard to get the academic qualifications necessary. For George Carey, his mind woke up when he encountered Christ, to the extent that he later studied for a doctorate and taught in three different theological colleges at various stages of his ministry. He provides a further illustration that where God calls, he equips.

This principle has a series of applications. For example, a Christian called by God to a political career will find strength and wisdom given to him or her to handle the demands of political life. A Christian called to be a home-maker and full-time parent will find strength from God to deal with the frustrations and burdens which that life brings. The pressures will be real in both cases, but so will the experience of the grace and power of God to meet them.

A significant question that arises is how to find out what God is calling each of us to do and to be. The next chapter will look particularly about this in terms of our main occupation in life, but for now we shall think about living with an up-to-date call from God.

LIVING UNDER THE ACTIVE SOVEREIGNTY OF GOD
'The Son can do nothing on his own, but only what he sees the Father doing; for whatever the Father does the Son does likewise,' said Jesus.[17] The New Testament scholar C. H. Dodd called this saying 'the parable of the son in the father's workshop', picturing the young Jesus learning from his father Joseph in the carpenter's workshop in Nazareth. Just as the boy Jesus learned his trade as a carpenter by watching his earthly father and copying what he saw, so Jesus the Son of God watched his heavenly Father at work and did what he saw his Father doing.

There is a principle of Christian living which Jesus models here, namely that a key to serving God is looking out for what he is doing, and being ready and willing to join in. We are to copy Jesus in this, for our mission is to be his: 'As the Father has sent me, so I send you,' Jesus told his disciples.[18] Looking for what God is doing and joining in operates at a number of levels.

There is the general level of being holy as God is holy (considered in chapter 4), which commits us to being ready for our characters to be moulded by God's Holy

Spirit to be like God's character: loving, patient, just, peace-loving, and so on. Our heavenly Father is at work in the world in ways that reflect his character and we need to mimic him. This has been the classic basis of Christian medical work and social concern and involvement, seeking to offer the love that the Father has for those in need, from the motive that people in need are loved by God and valuable to God.

More specifically, our spoken Christian witness will be affected by this principle. A key to spoken witness to our faith is looking for those in whom God is at work and seizing the moment. I have been involved in a number of missions, when a church or other Christian group has put on special events with the aim of introducing others to Christ. Always when I have visited the Christians with whom I was to work, I have encouraged them to look out for the surprising people in whose lives God is at work to draw them into faith in Jesus Christ.

I was helping at a week-long student mission some years ago and went into the college dining room for lunch on the first day of the mission. There was loud music going on and one man was dancing on the tables – he was known as a real 'life and soul of the party' type, who drank far too much and could be very loud and raucous. The Christians in the college were very surprised later in the week when that man responded to the message of Christ. A friend invited him to one of the mission meetings and he went along, heard the talk by the speaker, and prayed, asking Christ to come into his life. Beneath the loud and brash exterior was a spiritually hungry person with a real longing to know God in a personal way.

Someone who is seeking to live under the active sovereign power of God will be looking out for this kind of surprise from God. To that end we need to pray regularly for those we know, that God will give us opportunities to speak to them about Christ, and to be ready to take those opportunities when they come.

A further application of looking for what God is doing and joining in is seeking new paths that God may be opening for us. The motto of some Christians – and churches – seems to be 'as it was in the beginning, is now, and ever shall be', when God may have moved on to something else. There is an enormous reluctance in some churches to close down a group because it has served its purpose and something new needs now to be done. But this leaves churches with endless meetings which serve no real purpose. In this continuing search for God's purposes, there is no substitute for regular time spent consciously with God, individually and as a Christian body.

Nehemiah as an example
The Old Testament character of Nehemiah is a good example of keeping in touch with God and therefore being ready when God wants a new direction and a fresh move – and Nehemiah is not in a religious leadership role at all, but works in a king's palace as a servant. When we first meet him, he is the king of Babylon's cup-bearer or wine steward (Nehemiah 1.11). Within a short time he is governor-designate of Judea with a brief to rebuild the walls of Jerusalem (2.6). What has happened to change things, and why is Nehemiah able to say that, 'the gracious hand of my God was upon me' (2.8)?

Prayer
Nehemiah was a man who prayed. When Nehemiah hears news about the mess that the city of Jerusalem is in, his reaction is to turn to God and to pray (1.4–11). When he faces the most powerful man on earth, King Artaxerxes, and finds Artaxerxes asking what help he wants, he prays (2.4). As the book of Nehemiah goes on, in crisis after crisis, we find Nehemiah's first response is to go to God

and pray, such as when there are threats to the building work (4.7–9). Indeed, at times he records his prayers when he is under pressure (5.19; 6.14).

Nehemiah's initial prayer has many lessons for us. He comes to God with a fresh awareness of who God is, great and powerful, yet also loving and keeping his promises (1.5). He comes to God in repentance for sin, both his own and his people's (1.6–7), rather than trying to pretend that all is well. He comes to God in confidence, asking God to keep to the promises he has made (1.8–10), quoting from Scripture: 1.8–10 is a mosaic of quotations from the book of Deuteronomy.[19] He comes to God, finally, to ask (1.11). And this goes on for four months (1.1; 2.1).

These are all key factors in our praying, particularly in keeping our contact with God fresh and alive so that we are alert and listening when God speaks in some way to call us to something new. As we focus our attention on the greatness and tenderness of God, we shall be more 'in tune' with his purposes for the world and for our lives. As we understand our own sinfulness and failings and confess them to God, we shall receive the renewing forgiveness of God more and more. As we grow in knowledge of the promises of God in Scripture, we shall be better able to call on God's help when we need it. As we ask God persistently for a greater vision of his purposes, and a better grasp of our place in those purposes, we shall be in the right place at the right time for God to use us.

In some Christian circles prayer is often spoken of as important, but not actually practised. People *say* that prayer is vital, but in reality the programme of their church is long on activities and short on prayer. The lesson of Nehemiah is that *to pray is to act*, for prayer opens the situation to the most powerful and important adviser and changer of situations in the universe, God himself. To be regular and consistent in our prayers will make us more and more in tune with heaven's purposes.

Planning
Nehemiah did not only pray, not least during the four months that he had to wait before the king gave him the opportunity to go to Jerusalem. When Nehemiah first prayed (1.11) he was very vague about what he should do: it was over the four months that the conviction must have grown that he was to go and supervise the work himself (2.5). So when he had the opportunity to go, Nehemiah had his 'shopping list' at the ready: letters of safe conduct to provincial governors, and a letter to the keeper of the king's forest to provide the timber which he would need (2.7–8). He had thought through what would be needed and was ready with his requests.

Nehemiah's planning also appears later in the book. We have already seen that Nehemiah prayed when facing opposition (4.7–9): he also 'set a guard as a protection . . . day and night' (4.9). Rather than, on the one hand, be super-spiritual and pray and then sit back, or, on the other hand, rush around doing practical things and forget to pray, Nehemiah did *both*. His prayerfulness was not quietism that refuses to get its hands dirty.

Again, there are lessons here about responding to what you already know of God's purposes by action, and being ready to move into new action if the situation seems to demand it. Such action, like Nehemiah's, will need to be rooted in a life of prayer, and it will be focused on the goals which God regards as important. For Nehemiah the goal was to rebuild the city of Jerusalem both physically and spiritually.

LIVING WITH TODAY'S CALL FROM GOD

It is easy to be locked into yesterday's call from God to the exclusion of today's. Keeping open lines of communication with God is vital if we are to avoid this. An audit of your spiritual life may be helpful, talking over your walk with God with a trusted adviser or friend. For some, time away with God on retreat, with space and time to read the Scriptures and devotional books, to reflect and to pray, is a way of renewing this contact. Others cannot take such a path for family or other reasons and they will need to find ways of keeping in regular touch with their heavenly Father, so that their ears are increasingly tuned to his wavelength.

Living actively under God's sovereign power means a readiness to watch for him working and then to join in with enthusiasm. This will be important for Eric in facing his redundancy from the brick works. Otherwise, it would be easy for him to spring into action looking for a job, any job, without consciously opening himself up to the possibility that the redundancy is God's messenger, telling him to change direction. In this he will need the support and prayer of members of his church, as well as the advice of relevant people, such as the local job centre staff.

In the event Eric, who had left school at sixteen to take up his apprenticeship at the brick works, retrained as a primary school teacher. No one was more surprised than he was when the college offered him a place on the course, for he had never thought of himself as potentially a student at all. However, Eric found himself answering the question put to him at the job centre, 'What do you really enjoy doing?', by talking about the children's group he helped with on Sundays at church – and that was what led ultimately to the college course.

For Reflection

Take a piece of paper and draw a line representing your walk with God. It may be straight or, more likely, have diversions, bends, turns and the like in it. Then mark particular points of significance in the development of your life with God, using symbols or words to identify what was important at each point.

Think about the way that your understanding of God's call for you has grown and changed over the time on your drawing. What surprises you looking back? Are there any clues in the past as to what the next step might look like? You may find it helpful to talk this last issue over with a Christian friend or adviser whom you trust.

6   *Called to Do*

The fourth facet of vocation is God's call to serve him and our fellow human beings in particular tasks or roles. As we have already noticed, this is not the central focus of the New Testament's use of 'call', and we need again to underline the implications of the image of the various levels of a building for these different senses of 'vocation'. Without serious attention to the first three levels – the call to belong to Christ, the call to holiness and to a corporate life in the body of Christ, and the call to dependence on and trust in God – there is a good chance of getting this last level wrong. The top storey of a building will not be stable if the lower storeys are not solidly in place. Our personal encounter with God, our walk with God, our commitment to relationships within the people of God, and our consciously seeking the purposes of God, are all vitally important prerequisites to asking narrower 'vocation' questions about God's particular purposes for each of our lives.

Nevertheless these narrower questions need addressing and this chapter and the next offer a framework within which to tackle them. The 'way in' to this will be through a look at Paul, for all four of the New Testament uses of 'call' in connection with particular tasks or roles are to do with him. From there we shall draw a number of implications about vocation in connection with occupations and jobs in general, and so-called 'Christian work' in particular.

PAUL'S CALLING
Twice Paul describes himself as being 'called', and in both cases it is that he is 'called to be an apostle'.[1] This was the

heart of Paul's particular calling from God, to be the voice of God to those who did not yet know him, calling them to belong to Jesus Christ, particularly those who were not Jews by background. This calling is expressed in the words of Christ to Paul on the Damascus road, as recorded in Paul's description of his conversion when on trial before King Agrippa:

> I have appeared to you for this purpose, to appoint you to serve and testify to the things in which you have seen me . . . I will rescue you from your own people and from the Gentiles – to whom I am sending you to open their eyes so that they may turn from the power of Satan to God, so that they may receive forgiveness of sins and a place among those who are sanctified by faith in me. (Acts 26.16–18, cf. Acts 9.15; 22.21)

Although this calling to serve God as an evangelist among people outside Judaism came at the same time as Paul came to faith in Jesus Christ, Paul himself understood the two callings as distinct. He speaks in his letters of the calling to be a Christian separately from the calling to particular tasks or roles, as we have already seen (in chapter 3).

So for Paul the calling to be an apostle, sent by God to lead others to faith in Christ, became the mainspring of his life. It was this that motivated him and made him tick, so that he could later write, 'It is he [Christ] whom we proclaim, warning everyone and teaching everyone in all wisdom, so that we may present everyone mature in Christ. For this I toil and struggle with all the energy that he powerfully inspires within me.'[2] Paul put his heart and soul into the task that God had given to him, acknowledging that the power he received to do the task came from God in the first place.

But how did Paul's life's-work progress? It is worth noticing that there was a considerable time-gap between

Paul's conversion and his eventual travelling missionary work – probably some thirteen or fourteen years.[3] Let's consider how that time was spent.

The role of Barnabas

When Paul (then known as Saul) became a Christian, life was initially very difficult. He first spent some time in the desert regions of Arabia,[4] presumably to give himself time to reflect on the changes he would face now that he believed Jesus to be the Messiah. Imagine Paul as a new Christian reading a passage like the prophecy of the suffering servant[5] afresh – and other Old Testament passages which speak of the coming one promised by God – and recognizing Jesus Christ there!

After some time Paul returned to Damascus and spent some time preaching his new faith there.[6] In that city Ananias could vouch for Paul's genuineness as a Christian, which would have allayed the suspicions of the Christian group there; after all, this man who was now preaching about Jesus had come to the city to arrest and imprison those who believed in him!

Some time later, quite possibly about three years later,[7] Paul had to flee Damascus for his life, since there was a plot to kill him. Paul himself later described this plot and his own escape over the wall, hidden in a basket, and it must have stuck in his memory.[8]

This seems to have been the time when Paul first visited Jerusalem as a Christian,[9] and he was met with great suspicion and caution. The Jerusalem Christians had heard rumours about Paul's conversion, but were understandably worried about him being a 'double agent' within the church, appearing outwardly to be a Christian, whilst betraying Christians to the Jewish authorities on the quiet. The person who made a difference here was Barnabas, who took Paul to a small group of the apostles and told them the story of Paul's conversion and his preaching about

Christ.[10] This swung things around and the initial suspicions of the Jerusalem Christians were changed into warm welcome. They allowed and encouraged him to preach boldly about Christ, especially among Greek-speakers, but this only lasted a short time (just fifteen days), for Paul again had to flee for his life back to Tarsus, in his home territory of Syria and Cilicia.[11]

Quite how long Paul spent in Tarsus we do not know. But we do know what his next move was, and it was Barnabas again who was a key figure in the new work.[12] Barnabas is a figure of great quality from the early church: whenever we meet him he is acting in a positive, encouraging way; indeed, his name means 'son of encouragement'. We have already noticed his role in helping Paul find acceptance with the Jerusalem church. Now he was sent by the same church to check on what was going on in Antioch.

A number of the Jerusalem-based Christians had been forced to flee the city because of persecution, and their scattering led to the message about Jesus being much more widely known. One group had gone to Antioch and began to speak about Jesus not only to Jews, but also to Greek-speaking Gentiles. The results were remarkable – a new church had rapidly been born in the city. The Jerusalem church, which seems to have been the 'mother church' of this time, sent Barnabas to find out what was going on.

Barnabas was absolutely delighted with what he saw! He recognized that God was at work in the city and he stayed long enough to encourage and teach the church there, until it reached the point where large numbers were becoming Christians. Wise man that he was, Barnabas knew that he needed help to continue the work in Antioch – and Paul was the person he thought of to give that help, so he went to Tarsus and fetched him. The two of them taught and encouraged the new church in Antioch, spending over a year there.

The vital importance of Barnabas' encouraging work in the early stages of Paul's career as a Christian cannot be overstressed. It is thanks to Barnabas that we have the letters of Paul in our New Testament, as well as his great work in planting churches in strategically important cities of the Roman empire. Barnabas is a model of the call to 'provoke one another to love and good deeds . . . *encouraging one another* . . . all the more as you see the Day approaching'.[13] Barnabas shows the results of the mutual interdependence that is a consequence of our lives having been bound together by our common faith in Christ.[14]

The church in Antioch
If Barnabas provides a splendid model of the help an individual Christian can be to a brother or sister in hearing and responding to God's call, the young church at Antioch is a good example of the help a body of believers can give. The account of the church we have is brief, but packed with significant themes for understanding how God's call is experienced; and it provides the third New Testament example of 'call' in connection with a particular task or role:

> Now in the church at Antioch there were prophets and teachers: Barnabas, Simeon who was called Niger, Lucius of Cyrene, Manaen a member of the court of Herod the ruler, and Saul. While they were worshipping the Lord and fasting, the Holy Spirit said, 'Set apart for me Barnabas and Saul for the work to which I have called them.' Then after fasting and praying they laid their hands on them and sent them off. (Acts 13.1–3)

God the Spirit, through the church met together, spoke to call Barnabas and Paul to new work. Paul would have known the content of the call to 'the work to which I have called them', for he had understood since day one as a Christian what that work was to be; taking the Christian gospel to the non-Jewish world. But it was now, some thirteen to fourteen years after Paul's conversion, that God spoke to call him out into that work in a fresh way. This was the time when what is often thought of as Paul's life's-work began, his so-called 'missionary journeys' around modern Turkey and Europe.

Notice what *did not* happen here. It was not that the church in Antioch met together, agreed that Cyprus needed to hear about Jesus, and then asked for two volunteers to go to the island.[15] Nor was it that Barnabas and Paul felt concerned that the people of Cyprus should hear the Christian message, and therefore asked the church to support them in going to the island. What happened was that *God took the initiative*. The body of Christians at Antioch was the means through which God called Barnabas and Paul to this new work, but the impetus for the new move came from God himself.

In the New Testament the normal means through which God calls – in all the dimensions of the word that we have explored – is his people. The church is to be the ear that listens to God and the mouth that passes on what it hears.[16] These Christians in Antioch were serious about seeking God's purposes when they met together, for they not only prayed, but also fasted. They regarded finding what God wanted as more important than the food they ate, rather like Jesus' description of his own concerns: 'My food is to do the will of him who sent me.'[17] The church at Antioch really does seem to have put finding the purposes of God first, as the top priority of its life.

It is very striking to compare the New and Old Testaments on the means by which God calls to particular tasks, for in the Old Testament individuals such as Abraham, Moses, Isaiah, Ezekiel, or Jeremiah are usually called through personal encounters with God. This virtually never happens in the New Testament. Even Paul, who is often thought of as being like the Old Testament examples (because of his encounter with the risen Christ on the

Damascus road), is not an exception, for we see him here in Antioch receiving his call to new work through the church.

The reason for this contrast of Old and New Testaments lies in the gift of the Holy Spirit. On the day of Pentecost, Peter saw the giving of the Holy Spirit as fulfilling God's promise, 'In the last days it will be, God declares, that I will pour out my Spirit on all flesh.'[18] The gift of the Spirit to *all* believers is a major contrast between the old and new covenants. In Old Testament times the Spirit was given to particular people at particular times for particular tasks, whereas in New Testament times *every* Christian receives the Spirit, for it is through the Spirit's ministry that anyone can become a Christian at all. Therefore the body of believers meeting together is vitally important as a means of discerning God's call. In seeking and finding the call of God today, our brothers and sisters in Christ are going to be very important indeed.

How did the Spirit's call through the church come? Most likely it was through someone speaking as the church was 'worshipping the Lord and fasting' and telling the group what they believed God was saying. Such people in the early church were usually called prophets, and we meet them dotted about the New Testament. Their words were taken seriously, but their words were never accepted automatically as coming from God. They were always tested first by the church where they spoke, to see if it really was God speaking.[19]

That is what seems to have happened in Antioch, for the indications are that the commissioning, when the church prayed and laid hands on Barnabas and Paul before sending them off, took place after an interval, not immediately.[20] The church took time to pray and reflect, to see if what the prophet had said was from God. Doubtless the good fit of the prophet's words with what Paul already knew of God's purposes for his life was one factor in deciding that it was.

It cannot have been easy for the church at Antioch to release Barnabas and Paul to move on. They had both been key figures in the foundation and growth of the church there and they would leave a big gap. God's call to Barnabas and Paul needed a response of faith, not just by the two men but also by the church in releasing two of their most gifted leaders. The church had to trust God that he would provide what they needed in leadership and teaching without Barnabas and Paul around.

The call certainly needed a response of faith by Barnabas and Paul, for it was still very vague. They were to step out and go without any security other than the knowledge of God's call. Not for them a nice house, a good pension, and security for the future: their lives were now to be more like that of Abraham, who was called by God to leave his home country to go to another land which God promised to show him.

Any call from God to new work of any sort will need such a dual response of faith. Those called will need to trust in the God who has called them. The rest will need to trust in the God who is still their God and still concerned for them, that he will provide what is needed. There can be a tendency to believe that some people are absolutely indispensable to the life of a church; that if they move on, the hole they would leave would be too great. This cannot be true if we genuinely believe that the God who calls some to move on is also the God who provides for those whom he calls to stay.

Paul's puzzlement
The fourth and final use of 'call' in connection with particular tasks or roles comes from a later stage of Paul's life. By this stage he was an experienced missionary who had travelled widely in modern Turkey preaching about Christ and planting new churches. Having returned to some of the churches that he and Barnabas had planted, in order to

encourage and strengthen them in their faith, he then went through a time when he could not identify what God wanted him to be doing next.[21]

Paul, accompanied by Barnabas and Timothy, found every door slammed in his face. They went through Phrygia and Galatia, but the Spirit of God forbade them to preach the gospel there. They tried to enter the province of Bithynia, but God prevented them getting in. They travelled on and ended up in Troas, puzzled by then as to what God wanted.

This was not Paul's normal experience! His normal practice was to use the network of excellent Roman roads to get around, travelling to cities which were regional centres and proclaiming Christ there. Often he would stay some time in a place, such as the two years that he spent in Ephesus.[22] In Ephesus his strategic plan worked beautifully, for 'the whole province of Asia . . . heard the word of the Lord'.[23] Paul and his colleagues had not left the city; he had been speaking daily in a hired room in Ephesus. But because Ephesus was the regional centre, the capital of the province of Asia (the western part of modern Turkey), people came to the city to go to market and to do many other things on offer in a large city. It was on these visits that they heard Paul speaking about Christ and some of them came to faith. On returning to their home towns along the valley of the River Lycus they told their friends and neighbours about their new-found faith and churches were planted; this seems to be how the church in Colossæ began, through Epaphras, a native of Colossæ, who was one of Paul's converts in Ephesus.[24]

Ephesus represents Paul's usual method of working, whereas his experience in Acts 16 was very different. There God was deliberately stopping him going in certain directions, because there was a particular new step that God intended Paul to take: the gospel was to be preached in Europe for the first time. God told Paul about this through a vision of a Greek man asking Paul to help the Macedonian people. Luke, the author of Acts, was with Paul at the time, and records, 'When he [Paul] had seen the vision, we immediately tried to cross over to Macedonia, being convinced that *God had called us* to proclaim the good news to them.'[25] It is interesting that Luke uses the language of call here for a special new step in the progress of the Christian gospel through the Roman empire, probably because Paul and his friends were particularly conscious of God guiding them to take that new step.

Doubtless Paul and his companions had been praying and seeking God's will, and this vision came as the answer they were looking for. Quite possibly that group was the means God had used to prevent Paul entering Phrygia, Galatia, and Bithynia earlier, as one or other of them shared words that they believed God was saying to the group.

What emerges from comparing this experience of God's call to a new step with Paul's usual strategic plan is that Paul was open to God directing him in a different way. Paul had his normal method of working and kept going in that way unless and until God pointed him in a different direction.

Some Christians suffer from paralysis by analysis: they spend so much time thinking about what to do next that they never get on and do anything at all! The lesson from Paul's example is that we should use our minds in setting out in one direction, while remaining open to the possibility that God will redirect us. This is another application of the principle of looking for what God is doing and joining in (which we saw in chapter 5).

The danger in the way some other Christians think about God's guidance is that they treat the exceptions in Paul's experience as the norm. So they see this period in Acts 16 as putting forward what should be normal Christian experience of guidance by God: they expect 'supernatural' intervention, such as visions, or God obviously preventing them taking wrong paths, at every turn. This approach misses Paul's more usual method of working, typified by his ministry in Ephesus, which gives a place to the mind and planning, while remaining open to the sovereign direction of the Holy Spirit.

Gifts

Paul's approach to God's call to particular tasks or roles is closely related to his teaching on gifts.[26] This is a vast field which we cannot explore in detail, and we simply need to note one important distinction here.

The distinction is this: there are certain tasks that every Christian is expected to undertake, but which God specially equips some Christians to perform to a remarkable degree. Hospitality is a good example, for all Christians are called to be hospitable, to welcome others into their homes and to share their lives with neighbours and strangers.[27] But there are some Christians who have a particular ability to make visitors welcome and find special fulfilment in so doing. They will have people to meals, or to stay, at the drop of a hat; they seem to be able to make meals stretch endlessly. They are not fazed when people turn up unexpectedly. Those visiting their homes comment on how relaxing and refreshing it is to be there, and how valued and important they feel as visitors. Such people exhibit the *gift* of hospitality.

The danger is that the person with such a gift can assume that what they are doing is what any Christian could do. Peter Wagner calls this mistake 'gift projection':

> . . . the idea comes across that so-and-so did what he or she did simply because they loved God so much. Ergo, if you loved God that much . . . you could do the same thing. If you are not able to do these things, you now know the reason why. There is something deficient in your relationship with God.[28]

One result of this 'gift projection' is to induce guilt in those who are not gifted in that way. Such an approach panders to excessive individualism, rather than accepting that none of us has all the gifts. Indeed, God has designed things that way, for he wants us to learn interdependence by seeing our own weaknesses complemented by others' strengths.

A true grasp of Paul's teaching on gifts, which is part of his larger teaching on the knitting of Christians into the body of Christ, guards against such false guilt. It places the responsibility squarely on us to seek, find, and use our own God-giftedness, whilst protecting us against both jealousy of others' gifts and underrating our own.

This teaching about gifts is important for Clare in deciding about her public examination subjects, for a key issue that her youth leader will want to raise with her is what subjects she performs best in and finds interesting and satisfying. If God, in the way that he has created her, has equipped her in those ways, then she should carry those areas as far as she can. Clare found herself as a result taking French and Spanish, since she seems to have natural abilities in languages and enjoys the work involved. She wonders whether part of God's purposes for her, later in life, will be to live for some time in a country speaking one of those languages.

For Reflection

Think back to one particular 'change of direction' choice that you have made while you have been a Christian. What were the most important factors which led you to that choice? How far do they reflect the factors which were influential in Paul's case in the incidents discussed in this chapter?

Then think of some more day-to-day choices that you have made recently. How have you made them? How far do they reflect the factors which were influential in Paul's case in the incidents discussed in this chapter? Pray that God will increase your confidence and trust in him that he will lead you in the right paths in such choices.

7 Called to Work

Where do work and jobs fit into this picture? It is very noticeable that the biblical writers never identify calling with work and jobs in the way that some moderns do. Indeed, at one stage of his life Paul spent most of his time in what we might think of as a 'job' that was not the heart of his calling at all. That, as we have seen, was his responsibility to be an apostle to the Gentiles. But when he went to Corinth, for the first part of the time he was there, he had to earn a living by collaborating with Priscilla and Aquila, two fellow Jews, making tents.[1] Then on Saturdays, in his 'spare time', he went to the Jewish synagogue and spoke, trying to persuade his hearers to follow Jesus Christ.[2]

However, when Silas and Timothy arrived Paul switched to full-time proclamation work, teaching about Jesus all the time.[3] Silas had just come from Philippi, bringing a gift of money from the church there for Paul's support;[4] hence Paul was now free to devote the bulk of his time to his true calling, to evangelism, rather than having to earn his daily bread by his tent-making trade.

During the time when Paul had to make tents to keep himself financially afloat, he would, I am sure, have seen his tent-making as a worthwhile occupation. Nevertheless, he was probably itching to get on with his real calling, proclaiming Christ to others. At this time his 'job' (in our modern sense) of tent-making was not the focus of God's purposes for Paul. Paul's job and his calling were not necessarily the same thing.

A BIBLICAL VIEW OF WORK

We need, therefore, to understand work in its biblical context, and this means returning to the original purposes of God for humanity in Genesis 1–3.[5]

Work, creation and creativity

Work is part of the purpose of God for our race in creation, according to Genesis. This emerges explicitly in both of the creation stories in Genesis. In the first, God tells the man and the woman, '. . . fill the earth and subdue it; and have dominion over the fish of the sea and over the birds of the air and over every living thing that moves upon the earth.'[6] In the second, the man is given the task of tilling and keeping the garden.[7] Work is not a curse that fell upon our race because of our disobedience to God, but it is part of our nobility, our humanness, to be workers. We are given, under God, responsibility to steward the created order. Within this mandate comes a wide range of human activities: science, which seeks to understand the creation; farming and technology, which in different ways utilize the created world for our good; ecology, caring for and protecting the environment and creatures of God's world; the arts, expressing our human creativity, which reflects the creativity of God himself; and many, many more.

The creation stories demonstrate an implicit reason for believing that it is part of God's creation purpose for us to be workers, namely that he himself is a worker. Genesis 1 presents God as working to create the heavens and the earth and all that occupies them, and God at the end of his work expressed satisfaction and delight in the results of his toil: 'God saw everything that he had made, and indeed, it was very good.'[8] Humankind, made in God's image, is to be like him at this point, working and finding one of the main satisfactions of life in working. The parallel of humanity and God is made plain by the Ten Commandments, which stress that the pattern of resting from work one day in seven follows from God having rested one day in seven when he created the universe.[9]

Given the link of human work with God's creative actions, we ought to expect that our work will involve creativity too. So much work is dehumanizing because it has no element of creativity to it, with the result that the workers feel alienated from their work. This can be seen in some production processes in which the workers at one stage never have the satisfaction of seeing the results of their labours and being able to admire those results as 'very good'. We are designed to take delight in the results of our creativity, for this is part of being made in God's image. As Graham Dow puts it, 'Our creativity is the expression of God's creative being through the energy and command he has given us.'[10]

A good example of such creativity in work is Bezalel, who was equipped by God with artistic abilities and used these in the oversight of much of the embroidery, carving, design, stone-cutting, and metalwork needed for the Tent of Meeting, not least by sharing his skills in teaching them to others.[11] Interestingly, Bezalel is described, unusually for the Old Testament, as having been *called* to this work: his creativity was to be given to the place where God met with his people.

There is no sharp divide between work and leisure in the creation stories, for the garden where Adam is placed is already a beautiful garden before he is given the responsibility of being its gardener.[12] 'Leisure, in the sense of sheer enjoyment of what God has given . . . would seem then to be of the highest esteem in human life.'[13] And where work is as creative as the creation accounts envisage, rest is the proper and necessary opposite pole.

Work, sweat and toil
Of course, creativity is not the whole story, as the Genesis accounts also recognize. Through our disobedience to God

the original intentions of God for our race have been damaged and spoilt. They have not been totally effaced, nor damaged beyond repair, but the damage is real and continuing.

In the case of work, God tells Adam and Eve that the result of their disobedience to God will be that their responsibility of looking after the earth will become painful toil:

> cursed is the ground because of you;
> in toil you shall eat of it all the days of your life;
> thorns and thistles it shall bring forth for you;
> and you shall eat the plants of the field.
> By the sweat of your face you shall eat bread
> until you return to the ground. (Genesis 3.17–18)

There is therefore always an element, greater or smaller, of sweat and toil in human work because of our first disobedience to God. To romanticize work, as if all people should find work highly fulfilling all the time, is a gross error which will only lead to disillusionment for the many people whose work contains a large proportion of pain and sweat of the brow.

This means there will always be two messages coming from our work and from any human activity. There will be a message derived from our being made in the creative image of God, and there will be a message derived from our fallenness and sin. There will be God's goodness and our inclination to evil, side by side.

The two messages can be seen by considering farming as an example. The element of creativity and delight in the results of creativity can be seen in the harvesting of crops which will be of great value and benefit to human society. But the element of sweat and toil is all too evident, even with the help of modern technological aids. The farmer who works long hours to get the harvest in, fighting at times against disease and the elements, bears eloquent testimony to this, especially in parts of the two-thirds world where the help available to Western farmers is lacking.

WORK TODAY

Work and paid employment

An immediate consequence of our reflection on work in the creation stories is that work should not be equated with paid employment. Such an equation is a modern concept springing from the industrial revolution, when work became something not based in the home. Two centuries down the road this has led to the eventual downgrading of home-based forms of work, such as bringing up children or home-making, since work has become defined in terms of economic productivity. That is why unemployment (so-called) is experienced as such a curse in modern times, for we worship today at the altar of economic productivity.

Christians will want to resist this trend and to encourage those who see their calling from God to be to work in a sphere that is not economically productive, but which is providing a useful contribution to human society. Those who are full-time parents or home-makers are one obvious example of this, and they are people who need to be valued and encouraged to work in this way.

Christians will also be wary of simply equating work and vocation, which leads to workers expecting to find their entire fulfilment through their paid employment – an expectation that will never be satisfied. Human beings are not simply workers: they need other sides of their lives and personalities to develop in order to find real fulfilment.

Sweat and toil in work today

A second consequence of our reflection on work in the creation narratives is to ask where we can see the element of sweat and toil in work today. The industrial revolution has resulted in societies where work can be alienating and painful, dividing people from each other, such as workers and management. For many, the link between their small part of the process of production and the end product is tenuous, to say the least: they cannot recognize the product of their labours as 'very good'. It just seems a slog.

In any sphere of life, there will be a choice in processes of work between those which will encourage and strengthen human interconnectedness and those which divide people; and between those which allow the workers to see the results of their labours and those which so fragment the process that little delight in creativity is possible. Christians will want to encourage and support choices that lead to greater humanity in the processes of work, and will therefore be likely to involve themselves in the decision-making and negotiating over such things. Within the field of paid employment, they will do this both as management and workforce.

The demand for 'commitment' can be another form of sweat and toil, when the firm seeks to own its people body and soul. For a believer this can never be so, for we know that we ultimately answer to God and that there may be times when this higher answerability overrides our responsibility to our boss. We clearly need the help and advice of others in discerning when our employer is asking something which we should not give. But that our first and highest accountability is to God is beyond question for Christians.

Daniel provides a fascinating example of this kind of higher loyalty at work: each of the stories in the first six chapters of the Old Testament book of Daniel involves a clash of loyalties.

Daniel and his friends as young men in the pagan king's court face eating food that is not acceptable for reasons to do with their faith; they decline to do so and they grow healthier, stronger and more intelligent than the other students they are competing with (ch. 1).

Daniel is able to describe and interpret the king's dream, in spite of all the king's courtiers and magicians being unable to do so. Why? Because he and his friends have prayed to the 'God in heaven who reveals mysteries', who is able to reveal what the pagans' gods could not (ch. 2).

Shadrach, Meshach and Abednego, Daniel's friends, are thrown into the blazing furnace because they will not bow down and worship the king's golden statue, having told the king:

> If we are thrown into the blazing furnace, the God we serve is able to save us from it, and he will rescue us from your hand, O king. *But even if he does not*, we want you to know, O king, that we will not serve your gods or worship the image of gold you have set up. (Daniel 3.17–18, NIV: italics mine)

And, remarkably, God vindicates them by saving them in the furnace. But notice their approach: loyalty to their God counts for more than the value of their lives (ch. 3).

Nebuchadnezzar, a pagan ruler, is reduced to behaving like an animal because he believes his greatness to be something he has achieved entirely by himself. When he turns to God and acknowledges his arrogance, his reason returns and he rules his empire as before, but bows in worship and acknowledges the greatness of God (ch. 4).

Daniel interprets the writing on the wall for Belshazzar which tells the king of his forthcoming fall from power. The kingdom is to fall because the sacred cups and other vessels from the Jerusalem temple have been used in Belshazzar's feast, in which the participants praised gods of gold and silver, bronze, iron, wood and stone; an action which is symptomatic of Belshazzar's general failure to honour the one true God (ch. 5).

Daniel deliberately and publicly goes to pray, knowing that prayer to anyone except the king has been made illegal. But his loyalty to God is higher than his loyalty to the king, even though he is the king's number two. And God delivers Daniel from the den of lions, where he is placed for his crime (ch. 6).

In each story, the key issue is loyalty to God, encouraging the first readers of the book to trust God and put him first – presumably because they were under pressure in their day to give up faith in God, or at least to treat God as less important than other things. And again and again the book of Daniel says that God is to be trusted; even if it leads to laying down your life, he is to be put first.

The meaning of success
A third area of importance is how 'success' is to be measured. Too often the measure we are offered today is merely one of increasing affluence. This contrasts with the creation narratives, which suggest that *faithfulness to God's purposes* is a truer measure. How might this be seen?

Faithfulness to God's purposes might be seen in resisting a dehumanizing trend in the structure of the process of production in a factory and, better still, offering a positive alternative which gives many of the benefits sought, but without the alienating spin-offs.

Faithfulness to God's purposes might be seen in drawing attention to dishonesty or sharp practice, even at the cost of advancement or one's own position. Cameron Marr was in such a position. A Christian who was a merchant banker, he found himself as one of three people who blew the whistle on the manipulation of financial information for personal gain in the bank where he worked. The result was that he lost his job.[14] The cost of integrity can be high, but faithfulness to God is the highest value that a Christian has, the true measure of success.

Faithfulness to God's purposes might be seen in those who regard their service in a local church community to be so important that they decline promotion in their paid employment because of the extra demands it would make upon their time.

PERSONAL CALLING AND THE CHURCH

We have considered the application of some of these themes outside a 'church' context. Let's now turn our thinking to how they might look in a more avowedly God-honouring context, within the people of God.

Francis Dewar offers a fascinating analysis of 'vocation' in which he distinguishes three areas.[15] The first is the call to belong to Christ, in common with our thinking earlier. The second is the call to a task which is defined by others; this kind of call is characteristically mediated through an institution. Thirdly, there is what Dewar calls 'personal calling', by which he means something given to a person for him or her to do, which arises out of their uniqueness.[16]

A serious problem that he identifies is the confusion between the second and third sorts of calling in many people's thinking about ordination in the church and, we may add, in thinking more widely about so-called 'Christian work'. The confusion consists in the expectation that someone whom God is calling to be ordained can be recognized by their inner 'sense of call' to ordination. This confusion has been promoted by the question put to those being ordained in the Anglican ordination services, 'Do you believe, *so far as you know your own heart*, that God has called you to the office and work of a priest (or a deacon) in his church?' (italics mine). This question is easily understood to encourage the idea that the 'inner call' is what is vital in offering oneself for ordination.

Such confusion arises from the failure to recognize that ordination – and much 'Christian work' – is essentially a role defined by others. The church of God needs certain things to happen in order for it to stay true to its calling as the people of God; and the way of ensuring that these things happen is to appoint people to enable and equip the church in those directions. The tasks include leadership, teaching, evangelism, prayer, training, pastoring, counselling, and leading worship. Those chosen to do this must have the appropriate qualities and aptitudes for those tasks, but may or may not have a particular 'inner' sense that God is calling them to this task. Because the church needs those qualities and aptitudes, it appoints people whose responsibility it is to discern whether they are present. God's calling comes, therefore, through these people who are given the responsibility of such discernment. It is an external call, and not necessarily an internal one.

However, as Francis Dewar points out, if a minister has no personal sense of call in *any* area of life, something is very wrong. But the wrongness stems from the minister being a *Christian* who is failing to live out his or her personal response to God; not from the necessity that anyone called by the church to be ordained should have an inner 'sense of call'.

This same principle applies, suitably adapted, to other forms of so-called 'Christian work'. If a missionary society is seeking an accountant for a two-thirds world church organization, then the key requirements are to do with a person's technical abilities as an accountant and adaptability to work in another cultural setting. They may or may not have a strong inner 'sense of call' to the task, but it will be up to the missionary society's selectors to decide if they have the qualities and aptitudes needed.

Calling and the local church
Similar principles apply to the local church situation. When someone is needed to work with the children's groups in a church, the key questions will be to do with the person's Christian standing and personal experience of Christ, their personal circumstances (Have they got the time to give?, etc.), their ability to relate to children, and whether the person has at least the beginnings of the gifts necessary for

the particular task (which might be evangelism, teaching, or pastoring, to name but three). The skills of the task can often be learned 'on the job' if these things are present. By and large whether the person feels an internal compulsion towards the task is considerably less important in deciding what God wants. There needs to be an openness on the individual's part to the call of God coming through the people of God. The balance will be weighted towards the presumption that, if the people of God invite someone to undertake a task after due prayer and reflection, they are presumed to be right, unless there are very good reasons to the contrary. This goes against the grain of our modern Western individualism, but it is one of the points where our culture's values need to be challenged by the biblical emphasis on the Christian life as a *corporate* life.

Clearly there is the possibility that the church – whether local or wider – can get things wrong. Sometimes this can be by pointing an individual in the wrong direction. In such a case the person still has the responsibility to think through what is being proposed by the church before stepping out and acting. But even if people do go down an inappropriate path, they will not be written off by God for one mistake. He is more than capable of showing them – and others – that the path is inappropriate, and of bringing good out of the initial mistaken choice; and, indeed, of redirecting the person in a more appropriate direction.

It is also possible that the church can get things wrong by having too blinkered an approach. We saw that Gladys Aylward suffered from this in her day, when the missionary societies assumed that an uneducated woman could not be called by God to be a missionary in China. Christians need to work out in practice the belief that God is a creative God; his creativity is the same in the church as it is in the world at large. Looking at the world of nature we can see the enormous creativity of God, yet it is sadly possible for the people of God to produce an orderliness that is more like a graveyard than the riotous life and colour of creation. Sometimes this is why some Christians offer themselves for ordination: because they can see no other way of serving God in the church.

Anglicans (and I write as an Anglican) are particularly prone to this danger. The Church of England combines a highly centralized system of selection and training for ordination with a fairly bureaucratic approach to authorizing people to take responsibilities in the church's life; it seems almost that you need a licence from the bishop to arrange the flowers! A major factor in discerning gifts is allowing people to test out a potential area of giftedness. How, then, can someone test out many of the areas of public ministry if they require a licence from the bishop before they can ever preach or lead worship in the first place?

The fact that the God who created the world is the same God who calls his people into being should mean that we are open to God doing surprising things; open to him equipping surprising people to serve him in particular ministries; and open to changing the structures if they are restricting the life of the Spirit breaking through.

THE VOICE OF GOD THROUGH THE PEOPLE OF GOD

Critically important throughout our thinking are our relationships with our sister and brother Christians. It is they who will challenge us to stick at our 'secular' work, serving God in our job, or to stay with the sense that we should remain at home to support our children, or to try that college course that we never believed would be possible, or to talk to the minister about the possibility of being ordained. It is they who can offer us the resources of shared prayer and discussion in reviewing our service of God in all spheres. It is they who can sustain us through a difficult patch of serving God, in whatever area.

How can this happen? The key is being close enough to other Christians for them to be able to have this kind of input into your life and for you in turn to help them. Churches which have house groups meeting are one step down the road towards this level of fellowship, but only one step. Even where such fellowship groups do not exist, working alongside fellow Christians on a task, such as in the choir, on the church council, or in a churchyard gardening team, can begin to build the relationships that will make real interdependence possible. In every church the means need to be found to encourage the members in knowing and being committed to one another, so that real mutual encouragement and help in identifying appropriate spheres of service can develop.

The next stage involves taking a real risk, in someone sticking their neck out to acknowledge a need to others and ask for help. This can then unlock others to begin to do that too. It is moving from more academic, Bible study-oriented groups to groups where lives are really *shared*. This does not make Bible study irrelevant, as should be clear from the biblical examples we have considered throughout this book; but it means that Scripture becomes the book to which we look for God to speak to us and direct our lives, rather than being more like a textbook full of right answers to be learned in our heads. The Bible is to be *lived* in lives pursuing God's callings, in other words. Our final chapter will consider further how we can carry this into practice.

It was through a man in her church that Nancy was asked to get involved in a local drop-in centre for unemployed people. He heard that she was available and knew that the project needed someone with secretarial skills. Her training was used in two ways there: she helped people put together their CVs and fill in job applications; and she helped people learn how to use a word processor. She had wondered if she would be asked to become secretary to lots of committees, and dreaded the prospect, but was delighted with the opportunities given by the people-centred work of the drop-in centre. God had surprised her by the door that had opened.

For Reflection
1. Consider your main occupation in life, whether it is a paid job, college course, role at home or whatever. Where are the points of real fulfilment and real creativity in that occupation? Where are the points of 'sweat and toil'? How can you affect the situation to change things? (This may well involve doing something with others which you could not achieve alone.) Talk over your reflections on this with another Christian who is facing some of the same questions and pray for one another.
2. Who are the Christian people to whom you go when you need support or challenge or help in dealing with tricky issues? Think about how far you are able to help them – or others – in that way too. If you cannot think of anyone, ask God to give you eyes to see such people, and the chance to begin to share your life with them.

8 *How to Recover Calling*

The role of the Christian community in our understanding of our individual and corporate callings is considerable. But how is this to happen in practice? It would be too easy to stop at this point, having urged that it is vital for the health of the Christian body to recover the notion of calling or vocation, in the full and rounded sense we have seen. This chapter aims to provide realistic steps to be taken by a church which wants to work on that recovery process.

First, we shall summarize the benefits and the dangers of calling. Then we shall focus on three key elements that are necessary for the recovery of calling today: worship, teaching, and the body of Christ. In each case we are aiming to offer practical action that is achievable and that will make a difference.

THE BENEFITS OF CALLING

Four major benefits flow from the notion of calling as we have explored it. Each on its own is strengthening and powerful; taken together they are of immense value, both to the individual Christian and to the whole body of Christ.

Calling gives direction

Knowing something of my own calling provides great personal direction. It enables me to know what it means for *me* to belong to Christ, to be holy, to belong to the people of God, to be just, to be a peacemaker, and all the other general responsibilities that are mine as a disciple. It means that I can turn the main focus of my attention and energy in that direction and not feel at the mercy of every need that crosses my path.

The needs of the world are enormous, and without such a sense of personal direction a Christian can so easily be pulled this way and that by these many demands. Calling gives to individual Christians an understanding of the particular responsibilities for the world that God has placed on them. Such was the case with Jesus himself, for there were many sick in Israel whom he did not heal, many bereaved widows whose sons he did not raise from the dead, and many hungry people whom he did not miraculously feed. Nevertheless, he was able to say to God near the end of his life, 'I glorified you on earth by finishing the work that you gave me to do.'[1] Jesus completed his God-given mission by staying true to the direction his Father gave him.

An understanding of a person's calling will allow each Christian to serve God and other people without feeling false guilt about the needs he or she is personally unable to meet. This understanding leads to productive Christians who are not paralysed by the impossible aspiration to solve all the world's problems.

This is not a plea for lack of compassion in the face of obvious need that we may encounter. There are, of course, some occasions when God puts a need across our path that is not, at least at first sight, part of our personal calling; but it is part of our general Christian calling to be compassionate, to care for the needy and so on. So the notion of calling should not be used as an excuse for callous hard-heartedness; but neither should we let the great needs of the world overwhelm us.

Calling enables Christians to be distinctive
A second benefit of a thorough grasp of calling is that it gives us the ability to stand out from the crowd in a world where there are enormous pressures to conform. We thought about this earlier when we considered John Dean's

maxim from pre-Watergate times in the White House, 'To get along you have to go along.' In standing firm against the tide one key factor is a counter-rationale: that is, Christians do not, at the end of the day, belong to this world, but have a higher rationale for their existence, which is living to the glory and honour of God. This is what enabled Joseph to stand firm against the siren voice from Potiphar's wife, and it can enable Christian people today to stand out for Christ.

Calling provides perspective on the run-of-the-mill
Life is not always full of excitement and freshness. For everyone there are periods, longer or shorter, when life just goes on without some great new thing happening, when things are humdrum. An understanding of calling enables Christians to deal with these periods productively, rather than merely being frustrated by them. This is put beautifully in George Herbert's poem 'The Elixir', sometimes sung as a hymn:[2]

> Teach me, my God and king,
> In all things thee to see,
> And what I do in any thing,
> To do it as for thee.

> All may of thee partake:
> Nothing can be so mean,
> Which with this tincture (for thy sake)
> Will not grow bright and clean.

> A servant with this clause
> Makes drudgery divine:
> Who sweeps a room, as for thy laws,
> Makes that and th'action fine.

> This is the famous stone
> That turneth all to gold:
> For that which God doth touch and own
> Cannot for less be told.

Everything is to be done to the glory of God, for the whole of life is the arena of his concerns, not just the supposedly 'Christian' bits: even sweeping a floor can be done as an expression of discipleship.

For example, a good friend of mine is presently a full-time mother bringing up two small children, and at times she feels the frustrations of that lifestyle acutely. She has a university education, speaks a foreign language fluently, and holds considerable responsibility in her church. Had she chosen to do so, she could doubtless have developed a career very successfully. Unprompted, she commented to me that she at times reminds herself that she has been *called* (her word) to the task of bringing up children. When I asked further, she explained that this sense of calling is what enables her to survive the 'down side' of the experience of parenting – the sense that what she is doing in bringing up her children is of immense value to God and is making a real contribution to society.

Such a situation displays the benefit of a grasp of calling, enabling us to handle the run-of-the-mill without being totally frustrated by it.

Calling helps to balance sacrifice and fulfilment

The emphasis in the business world today is increasingly on positive styles of management and work development, so that individuals can find real fulfilment in the work they do. This goes with an encouragement of ambition, the desire to progress, that is common in such circles. This kind of thinking has infiltrated Christian circles in, for example, teaching about gifts which encourages each Christian to expect that all of their service for God will be highly fulfilling.

A previous generation of Christians had a different emphasis, centred on *sacrifice*. Christians were encouraged to be doormats, to lay down their lives and not to seek promotion or so-called 'worldly success'. The heroes who were held up were those who gave their lives to the mission field at the expense of a career, such as C. T. Studd, who studied at Cambridge and played cricket for England, but gave all that up to be a missionary in China.

Balancing the two concerns of fulfilment and sacrifice, both of which are proper and right, is not easy. Ambition in itself is not un-Christian, as can be seen by some of the language used in the New Testament, which speaks of the desire for progress and moving on. The despising of ambition comes from outside the Bible.

Unbridled ambition is, of course, a different thing, and that is where an understanding of calling can bring together ambition and sacrifice, fulfilment and surrender. In any sphere, to follow an ambition will involve a certain amount of sacrifice, but it can be borne because of the knowledge of a calling to that sphere. The cost can be paid in the understanding that there will, somewhere along the line, be fulfilment.

Similarly, an understanding of calling helps us to be realistic about the costliness of a path, so that we do not expect to receive only good things from it. Christians will never look at life through rose-tinted spectacles. A grasp of calling means that we can face the cost because of our highest ambition, which is to serve and glorify God, and that will also restrain our earthly ambitions within godly and appropriate limits.

THE DANGERS OF CALLING

The benefits of a good understanding of calling are great, as we have seen. But there are attendant dangers too, and these need to be watched in developing a church life that aims to appropriate the benefits of calling.

Over use

'Vocation' is used today with a wide range of meanings, and this book has been a sustained argument for the continuing use of the term with a specifically Christian content. However, there is a danger in making everything part of calling – the result can easily be that the word is effectively emptied of its meaning.

To see this, take a parallel example, the word 'mission'. The whole of a church's life can become described by the buzz-word 'mission', with the result that everything is to be seen as mission. The side-effect is that such a church often loses sight of a more narrowly conceived sense of mission: God reaching out in love to a world in rebellion against him.

The same can happen, in some circles, with the correct observation that the New Testament writers do not limit 'worship' to what happens in church: indeed, they use it of serving God in the whole of life. The danger with such an all-embracing use of the term is that what happens when Christians meet together is treated as though it is no different from the rest of life, and the meetings of such a church can be sloppily run and casual as a result.

Therefore, the use of 'vocation' or 'calling' will need careful definition in each case, so that it does not become yet another empty slogan in church life.

Exploitation

A second danger is the abuse of 'calling' to exploit others. For example, the nineteenth-century slave-masters in the United States used the idea of calling to underpin their belief that the black slaves had been given their station in life by God. The slaves were then told to follow their God-given calling, which meant they were to work their fingers to the bone for the benefit of their rich white masters. The idea of calling was being abused to reinforce injustice, rather like the (now censored) verse of the hymn 'All things bright and beautiful', which reflected such Victorian values:

> The rich man in his castle,
> The poor man at his gate,
> God made them, high or lowly,
> And ordered their estate.

Nowadays we Western Christians can see these blind spots of previous generations. What *we* need are sister and brother Christians from cultures other than ours who can help us to see our blind spots in understanding and applying calling to our situation, so that we do not end up exploiting others in the name of vocation.

Equating calling with work and jobs

A third danger in speaking in terms of calling is the false conclusion that, because the idea of calling *includes* work and jobs, it should be used *exclusively* of work and jobs. As we have seen, the heart of Paul's calling was not the same as his 'job' as a tentmaker. Indeed, it seems likely that it will be only a fortunate few who have a paid occupation which focuses on the heart of their calling. This is inevitable in the light of biblical realism about the all-pervasiveness of the effects of our rebellion against God. All of our occupations will consist, as we have seen, partly in calling and partly in the consequences of our fallenness and rebellion.

Of course, Christian people are responsible for seeking to combat the damaging effects of the fall in their work situations, many of which will be hard places to serve God. The workplaces of those in paid employment need the preserving and provoking presence of Christians (as salt) and their determination (as light) that truth and honesty should prevail.

Nevertheless, the equating of calling or vocation with work and jobs, which is very common today, can lead to the worship of work in the place of God. This might take the form of the Marxist version, which sees human beings as *homo faber*, simply economic units of production, or the version produced by the so-called Protestant work ethic (which is neither Protestant nor ethical, in my view), which leads to people's whole lives being consumed by their paid employment, to workaholism. The results that follow can be devastating, particularly when someone ceases to be economically productive, whether permanently – in retirement – or semi-permanently, through becoming unemployed. Equating their calling with their particular job can mean that their identity becomes entirely bound up with their job. By contrast, to see a particular job as *part* of God's calling for a person frees that individual, when the job ends (for whatever reason), to use the gifts they brought to the job in another sphere, perhaps on a voluntary basis when they retire.

The expectation that we shall find our entire fulfilment in life through paid employment, with the devastating effects this has on people's sense of value when they are not 'in work', is without question one of the greatest abuses of the theme of vocation.

RECOVERING CALLING TODAY
In recovering the rounded biblical understanding of calling that we have discovered, three areas of church life will be particularly important.

Worship
The evidence of both the Old and New Testaments suggests that an understanding of an individual's calling often comes in the context of worship, that is, during time spent consciously focused on 'engaging with God'.[3] Two examples illustrate this, Isaiah and Paul.

Isaiah was in the Jerusalem temple when he had the remarkable vision of God through which he received his call to be a prophet.[4] Quite possibly he was there attending one of the Israelite festivals,[5] and as the events of the festival went on God met him in a vision and Isaiah responded with the famous, 'Here am I; send me!'

Paul and Barnabas heard their call to a new area of work through the worship of the church at Antioch,[6] as we saw earlier (chapter 6). This call began with the initiative of God and was focused by God speaking through his people – most probably a prophet – in order to send Barnabas and Paul to speak about Christ, initially in Cyprus and then further afield.

Because God seems to have used times when his people were worshipping together as a body to call Christians to particular tasks, churches need to allow space to hear God speak in this way. This can happen in a number of ways, such as through an impression that someone gets that they (or someone else) should pursue a particular course of action, through the preaching at a church service, through the Scripture readings, or through the prayers.

There also need to be connections between what goes on when Christians meet together and what people experience in their daily lives and occupations. For example, Richard Higginson draws attention to the pattern of the praying that goes on in most church services, whereby some occupations are prayed for quite often, some occasionally and many never at all.[7] His list of examples is:

> *Quite often:* Nurse, teacher, politician.
> *Occasionally:* Ambulanceman, farmer, policeman, soldier, union leader.
> *Never:* Bank manager, broadcaster, corporation chairman, design engineer, salesman, solicitor.

This list could obviously be greatly expanded, but the basic point is clear. Our churches, by the kinds of occupations we pray for, are giving a message loud and clear about the kinds of work God is concerned about, mostly the so-called 'caring professions', along with those involved in politics and power, especially at times of national crisis. A church which is concerned to develop a wider understanding of vocation amongst its members could do worse than widening the scope of its intercessory prayers as a first step.

As a second example, some churches have begun to develop whole services which celebrate people's work. A church in Coventry ran a series of services over a period of time with the title 'My Work is God's Work', each led by one group of workers within the congregation. The group met to plan the service; they provided an exhibition in the church building of what they produced in the course of their work; they were involved at least in helping prepare the sermon, and sometimes in actually delivering it; and they would symbolically offer their work to God at some point in the service. The groups involved included those from the car industry, medicine, the law, education, and others.

Richard Higginson describes a parallel idea, of the adaptation of the central thanksgiving prayers of the eucharist (or communion service) to reflect the themes of work. Quoting from the work of an ordinand, he offers a proper preface, words for use at the breaking of the bread, an invitation to receive the bread and wine, a thanksgiving after communion, and a blessing.[8]

Such services give the message that there are connections to be made between our faith and our working lives, that God is involved in our daily occupations. This may be a significant factor in helping Christian people to see the whole range of occupations as potentially callings from God, and not just the obviously 'religious' ones of the ordained ministry, missionary work, or the life of a monk or nun.

Teaching
The need for teaching to help recover the meaning of calling covers four related points. First, the lack of actual teaching on God's call given in most churches is very

marked. It is quite possible to go for a year or longer and never hear the topic mentioned from the pulpit, let alone in house groups. The impression people receive is that the totality of being a Christian at work is turning up on time, not stealing the biros from your workplace, and trying to witness to Christ among your workmates.

There is therefore a crying need for preaching that addresses such issues. It may be that ordained ministers are not the best people to preach on such issues and that laypeople should be invited to speak about the issues they face and their Christian responses to those issues. Alternatively, the clergy will need to talk with the members of their congregations about the issues they face in serving God in their workplaces and feed those issues into their preaching. Indeed, ministers could be encouraged to visit some of their church members in their workplaces, to experience for themselves something of what it is like, especially now that 'work shadowing' has become acceptable.

Second, consider what kinds of people are used as the models of the Christian life in the sermons that you hear and the Christian books that you read. Is it not true that almost all are people engaged in so-called 'Christian work', often missionaries or ministers? The hidden message given by this kind of preaching is that, if you really want to serve God wholeheartedly, you need to go into an occupation like this.

The corrective to this imbalance is to provide models of Christian living in illustrations in sermons and in Christian books which show people serving Christ at work, or in parenting, or in other spheres. If we really believe that the whole of life is God's concern, then the illustrations in the preaching in our churches should reflect that belief. This book has sought to begin the task of finding such examples, but there are many more to be found.

Third, teaching about vocational issues needs to come at the right time. Teaching about good principles of marriage can be useful to a couple on the edge of separation; but how much better to teach them such principles during their wedding preparation! Similarly, younger people in our churches in the 13–25 age bracket are those who need to learn about calling, since this is the stage when they take many major life-shaping decisions, beginning with the decision as to which subjects to study for public examinations when they are sixteen. This is therefore the period when the possibilities need to be opened up with Christian young people, offering them help in seeing their lives from God's perspective and assisting them in making choices about the steps they must take.

For example, many young people are prepared for confirmation (in Anglican and Methodist churches, or the equivalent preparation for adult church membership in other denominations), but hear nothing at all in their preparation time about serving God in the world of work or as a parent. The classes are most often taken up with Christian beliefs and church practices – which are important – without making connections with the daily lives of the young people. Is this one reason why so many young people never darken the door of a church again after their confirmation classes: that it all seems irrelevant to their daily lives?

Fourth, in speaking to young people about serving God with their lives, it is clearly important that the need for more people in the ordained ministry and serving in other lands and cultures is presented, but never on its own as the only way of serving God fully and wholeheartedly. Alongside those needs young people should be encouraged to consider the need for Christians in journalism, education, politics, medicine, home-making and parenting, engineering, and many other fields, at all levels, influencing society in godly directions. The vision of Jesus, that his followers would be salt, preserving the good things within society and holding off the bad, needs to be the backcloth to this presentation of the ways to serve God in later life.

The body of Christ

Underlying our thinking throughout this book has been the key role of the church in seeking and finding God's calling for our lives. We have seen that it is regularly through the people of God that callings are heard and responded to. Four practical steps in the life of a church could enable this to happen better.

First, an adult Christian education programme needs to be developed. By this I mean the need to help adult Christians to grow in understanding of their faith and to learn to apply it in daily life. In this the preaching of our churches will be one important factor, and I have suggested ways in which sermons could begin to relate to people's everyday experience better.

But preaching is only one way of learning, and other forms of learning need to be used, especially forms that involve the learners themselves in the process of learning, through discussion, question and answer, thinking out case studies, and other ways. For some (larger) churches, their regular house groups may provide an arena to do this. For other churches a special series of meetings (for example, during Lent) may provide such an opportunity. Sometimes a group of churches may want to work together to share their resources to tackle such questions, or set up a teaching day with a visitor to stimulate people's reflections. No grandiose schemes are being suggested here, but the need for the connection to be made between faith and life is vital, and we need to find more and better ways of helping people to make that connection.

Second, churches need to develop real interdependence, a real sharing of lives. This building of relationships is vital if church members are really to be able to help each other in seeking and finding more of God's call on their lives. We trust people we know reasonably well, and without such trust we are unlikely to ask for their help, or to receive it if it is offered to us.

For many churches a group (or groups) meeting to pray together will assist that process, particularly if the leader is able to share some of his or her own struggles and to ask for the group's prayers. As the leaders of such groups become vulnerable in sharing their weaknesses and needs, others will begin to share themselves too. Again, house groups can assist such a process, provided they are groups where people really can meet at their points of need and weakness, rather than just being places where people wear masks of invincibility and infallibility all the time.

The tone that the leadership of the church sets in this regard will be very important. If those in overall charge give the impression that you have to be perfect (or nearly so) to follow Christ, people will hide their problems and weaknesses. If the leaders share their own weakness and point people towards the power of Christ to strengthen them and keep them going, the atmosphere can be very different.

Third, there is the need both to sustain and restrain one another in our discipleship, both of which depend on the quality of our relationships in the body of Christ. We shall need to sustain and strengthen a person or group when we believe that they are going in a direction that fits with God's call on their lives. This may involve practical support, even financial support, in helping them to go with God's purposes for them. Os Guinness cites the example of a member of a Christian group in Denver who was a total misfit in his job but did not believe that he could ever succeed at the work he really longed to be in. The group got together and provided three months' salary for him to enable him to make the change, because they recognized that his work did not express his calling from God and they wanted him to live in a way that did express that call.

The flip side of sustaining one another in pursuing our callings from God is that at times we will need to restrain each other. At times we will need to challenge each other as to whether we are pursuing a course that is really consistent with our calling, both our general Christian calling and our personal calling. This needs doing with care and sensitivity, but at times it will be the word of a sister or brother Christian that will hold an individual or a group back from disobeying God. Not to be ready to do this is to ask for trouble in seeing lives derailed from God's purposes.

A PICTURE

Os Guinness describes a painting in Neufchatel in Switzerland by Paul Robert, which is of the second coming of Christ. In the painting the people of a Swiss canton are rising into the air to meet Christ, each carrying in their arms the fruits of their callings: doctors who have healed people, architects who have created environments, and many others. In their faces can be seen both expectancy and a knowledge that they must answer to Christ for their stewardship of their callings.

This beautifully depicts the broad sweep of calling that we have considered. Nothing will be more powerful in our world today, in persuading our contemporaries that the Christian faith is worth considering, than Christian people living their lives wholeheartedly for Christ in every sphere. Such Christians live knowing that they are accepted by God solely because of Jesus' death on the cross (and so the pressure to achieve in order to be accepted is off) and knowing also that they must answer to God for the quality of their response to his call.

For Reflection

In the light of this chapter, what are the strengths and the weaknesses of your church's life in helping the congregation to seek and find their callings from God? Think about the practical steps that need to be taken in order to make the good areas better and the weak areas strong. How could these steps be put into practice? (This may well involve thinking and action by more than one person, and you should also consider who else needs to be involved and in what ways.)

Notes

1 Vocation?
1 Anthony Freeman, *God in Us: A Case for Christian Humanism* (SCM Press 1993). See the review in *Anvil*, vol. 11, no. 1 (April 1994) by Andrew Moore for a critique.
2 John White, *People in Prayer* (IVP 1978), pp. 131–2.
3 Isaiah 57.15; 55.8–9.
4 Genesis 1.28.
5 Psalm 111.2.

2 Call in the New Testament
1 Leviticus 11.44.
2 1 Peter 2.12.
3 Romans 8.31.

3 Called to Belong
1 Mark 3.13–19.
2 Acts 2.38–9.
3 Genesis 3.9.
4 Revelation 1.9–20.
5 Acts 10.
6 e.g. Romans 9.24; 1 Thessalonians 5.24.
7 2 Thessalonians 2.13–14.
8 1 Timothy 6.12.
9 e.g. Acts 2.38; 10.48; 19.5.
10 The responses are made by parents and godparents when the candidate is an infant.
11 This is particularly clear in the case of infant baptism, where the child is not able to take the initiative.
12 John McCarthy and Jill Morrell, *Some Other Rainbow* (Bantam Press 1993), p. 66.
13 Hebrews 9.15.
14 Revelation 19.9, my translation.
15 Philippians 3.14.
16 Lawrence and Diana Osborn, *God's Diverse People* (Daybreak/ Darton, Longman & Todd 1991), p. 56.

4 Called to Be
1 Ephesians 4.1, my translation.
2 1 Thessalonians 2.12, my translation.

3 2 Peter 1.10.
4 2 Peter 1.5–7.
5 2 Peter 1.3.
6 1 Peter 1.15.
7 Genesis 39.9.
8 e.g. Psalm 23.3.
9 Psalm 66.18–19.
10 I owe this example, and a number of other key ideas on vocation, to Os Guinness' tape 'Dreamers of the Day: Vocation'.
11 1 Corinthians 1.9.
12 N. T. Wright, *The Epistles of Paul to the Colossians and to Philemon* (Tyndale NT Commentary: IVP 1986), p. 143.
13 Acts 9.26–8.
14 Acts 11.22–6.
15 Acts 13.1–3.
16 Romans 15.7.
17 Acts 6.1–7.
18 *The Alternative Service Book 1980*, p. 371 § 15.
19 Galatians 6.2; James 5.16; Romans 12.10.
20 1 Corinthians 12.26.
21 Acts 20.18–35.
22 This is the most likely understanding of the Greek in Ephesians 4.11.

5 Called to Let God Be God

1 Acts 10.18.
2 1 Samuel 1.20; Exodus 2.10.
3 Isaiah 7.3; Matthew 1.21.
4 Genesis 17.4–6.
5 Genesis 2.19–20.
6 1 John 3.1.
7 David Jackman, *The Message of John's Letters* (IVP 1988), p. 81.
8 Matthew 5.9, 19.
9 Romans 4.17.
10 Genesis 1.6–7, 9, 11, 14–15, 24, 29–30.
11 Romans 11.29.
12 Ephesians 1.14.
13 The period is well described in Roy Coad, *Laing: The Biography of Sir John W. Laing, CBE (1879–1978)* (Hodder & Stoughton 1979), chapter 3.
14 Philippians 3.13–14; 4.12.
15 Mark 14.4–5.
16 Quoted in Alan Burgess, *The Small Woman* (Pan 1972, rev. edn), p. 250.

17 John 5.19.
18 John 20.21.
19 Nehemiah 1.8b = Deuteronomy 28.64; Nehemiah 1.9 = Deuteronomy 30.1–5; Nehemiah 1.10 = Deuteronomy 9.29.

6   Called to Do
 1 Romans 1.1; 1 Corinthians 1.1.
 2 Colossians 1.28.
 3 See F. F. Bruce, *Paul: Apostle of the Free Spirit* (Paternoster 1977), p. 475.
 4 Galatians 1.17.
 5 Isaiah 52.13–53.12.
 6 Luke's version of the story in Acts 9.1–25 appears to be 'edited highlights'. Fitting it together with Galatians 1.13–17, it seems most likely that the visit to Arabia recorded in Galatians occurred very shortly after Paul's conversion and before the preaching recorded in Acts 9.20.
 7 cf. Galatians 1.18.
 8 2 Corinthians 11.32–3; cf. Acts 9.23–5.
 9 Galatians 1.18; cf. Acts 9.26.
10 Acts 9.27.
11 Acts 9.29–30; Galatians 1.21.
12 The story of Paul's move to Antioch is told by Luke in Acts 11.19–26. F. F. Bruce, *Paul: Apostle of the Free Spirit* (Paternoster 1977), pp. 127, 133, suggests that the 'silent period' lasted about ten years, so that Paul would have been a Christian for some thirteen years when Barnabas fetched him to go to Antioch.
13 Hebrews 10.24–25.
14 See chapter 4.
15 Barnabas and Paul's first destination: Acts 13.4.
16 I owe the phrase to Professor C. F. D. Moule.
17 John 4.34.
18 Joel 2.28, quoted in Acts 2.17.
19 See 1 Corinthians 14.29 and 1 John 4.1 for Paul and John's instructions on testing the words of prophets.
20 Acts 13.3.
21 Acts 15.36–16.10.
22 Acts 19.1–21.
23 Acts 19.10, my translation.
24 Colossians 1.7; 4.12.
25 Acts 16.10, italics mine.
26 Particularly, see Romans 12.1–7; 1 Corinthians 12–14; Ephesians 4.1–16; 1 Peter 4.10–11.

27 e.g. 1 Peter 4.9.
28 C. Peter Wagner, *Your Spiritual Gifts Can Help Your Church Grow* (Marc 1979), pp. 53–6.

7 Called to Work

1 Acts 18.1–3.
2 Acts 18.4.
3 Acts 18.5.
4 2 Corinthians 11.9 and Philippians 4.15 make it clear that the Philippian church was the only one that supported Paul in his early work in Macedonia, where Corinth was. Philippians is a thank-you letter to the church for their gifts.
5 I am very grateful to Bishop Graham Dow for his advice and help on this question. See his 'What Place Does Work Have in God's Purpose?' in *Anvil* 1 (1984), pp. 139–51, in which he suggests that the pattern found in Genesis 1–3 is reflected in the ministry of Jesus and the vision of heaven also.
6 Genesis 1.28.
7 Genesis 2.15.
8 Genesis 1.31.
9 Exodus 20.8–11.
10 Graham Dow, 'What Place Does Work Have in God's Purpose?', p. 148.
11 Exodus 35.30ff.
12 Genesis 2.9–14.
13 Graham Dow, 'What Place Does Work Have in God's Purpose?', p. 143.
14 Cameron Marr, 'Keeping Faith in the City' in *Third Way*, vol. 16, no. 9 (December 1993), p. 15.
15 Francis Dewar, *Called or Collared? An Alternative Approach to Vocation* (SPCK 1991); see also his 'Consider Your Call' in *Theology* 88 (1985), 461–6.
16 His book *Live for a Change* (Darton, Longman & Todd 1988) offers a stimulating set of exercises to use in pursuing one's own personal calling.

8 How to Recover Calling

1 John 17.4.
2 Verses 1 and 4–6 from *The Poems of George Herbert* (Oxford University Press 1961), pp. 175–6.
3 I owe the phrase to David Peterson's stimulating study of worship in the Bible, *Engaging with God* (IVP 1992).
4 Isaiah 6.

5 Suggested by John Mauchline, *Isaiah 1–39* (SCM Press 1962), p. 89.
6 Acts 13.1–3.
7 See Richard Higginson, *Called to Account* (Eagle 1993), p. 244.
8 In his *Called to Account* (Eagle 1993), pp. 253–4.

Resources for Further Thought and Action

Out of the growing number of books and study materials on topics covered by this book, the following are some that I have found helpful. They are organized by the chapters, but some would fit more than one area.

General
Os Guinness has given a very helpful lecture 'Dreamers of the Day: Vocation' (ref. C2/10), obtainable from the Christian Impact tape library at: Christian Impact, St Peter's Church, Vere Street, London, W1M 9HP.

3   Called to Belong
These are books that would be particularly helpful for those starting out in the Christian life:

Michael Green, *New Life, New Lifestyle* (Hodder & Stoughton 1993: rev. edn).
John White, *The Fight* (IVP 1977).

The following introduce the Myers-Briggs Type Indicator, the measure of personality discussed:

Malcolm Goldsmith and Martin Wharton, *Knowing Me – Knowing You: Exploring Personality Types and Temperaments* (SPCK 1993).
Lawrence and Diana Osborn, *God's Diverse People* (Daybreak/Darton, Longman & Todd 1991).
Ian Williams, *Prayer and My Personality* (Grove Spirituality series no.20: Grove Books 1987).

4   Called to Be
Jim Packer's classic *Knowing God* (Hodder & Stoughton 1973) has much wisdom to offer on living a holy, distinctive life, particularly chapters 18–22.
CPAS publish an excellent study course and tape for churches wanting to explore spiritual gifts, which has good material about mutual support and encouragement. Both are called *Tools for the Job* and can be obtained from: CPAS Sales, Athena Drive, Tachbrook Park, Warwick, CV34 6NG (tel. 0926 334242).

5   Called to Let God Be God

The following are helpful on different areas of developing your own walk with God:

Richard Foster, *Prayer* (Hodder & Stoughton 1992).
Richard Foster, *Celebration of Discipline* (Hodder & Stoughton 1980).
Joyce Huggett, *Listening to God* (Hodder & Stoughton 1986).
Jane Keiller, *Patterns of Prayer* (Daybreak/Darton, Longman & Todd 1989).
John White has written an excellent study of Nehemiah as a leader, *Excellence in Leadership* (IVP 1986) which repays reading. It could be used in personal Bible reading, as it goes through the book of Nehemiah section by section.

7   Called to Work

Richard N. Bolles, *What Color is Your Parachute? A Practical Manual for Job Hunters and Career-Changers* (Ten Speed Press 1993: a new edition is published each year) tackles job-hunting and career changing very helpfully, working from within a Christian framework. A book with lots of practical help, checklists and exercises to do.
Francis Dewar, *Live for a Change* (Darton, Longman & Todd 1988) is a stimulating collection of practical exercises for exploring his idea of 'personal calling'.
Francis Dewar, *Called or Collared? An Alternative Approach to Vocation* (SPCK 1991) does the same job for those thinking towards ordination.
Richard Higginson, *Called to Account* (Eagle 1993) is a valuable pioneering book seeking to apply the key themes of Christian theology to the world of business. Dr Richard Higginson is Director of the Ridley Hall Foundation, which offers resources and courses for Christians working in business. For more information write to him at: Ridley Hall Foundation, Ridley Hall, Cambridge, CB3 9HG.
John Stott, *Issues Facing Christians Today* (Marshall Pickering 1984); chapters 9–10 offer stimulating thoughts on work, unemployment and industrial relations.
St John's Extension Studies (which offers excellent correspondence-course study materials for Christians) has a very good unit on 'God and the World', a major component of which is thinking about your work from God's perspective. Write to: St John's Extension Studies, Bramcote, Nottingham, NG9 3DS.
If you are considering ordination in the Anglican Church, CPAS Vocation and Ministry offer excellent resource sheets, weekend conferences, a regular newsletter and much other help. Write to: CPAS Vocation and Ministry, Athena Drive, Tachbrook Park, Warwick, CV34 6NG. Other resources are also available from the Advisory

Board of Ministry, the official body which advises the bishops on selection and training: The Vocations Officer, ABM, Church House, Great Smith Street, London, SW1P 3NZ.

8 How to Recover Calling

John Stott, *I Believe in Preaching* (Hodder & Stoughton 1982) (especially chapter 4, 'Preaching as Bridge-Building') offers some wise words on preaching that makes real connections with people's lives.

Also published by

TRI/\NGLE

FACING ANXIETY
by Roy Ward

An exploration of the causes of anxiety and its effects on our lives. Roy Ward offers practical suggestions for coping with anxiety.

UNDERSTANDING FRIENDS
How to get the best out of friendship
by Alistair Ross
Foreword by David Atkinson

Alistair Ross examines the many complex and fascinating questions involved in our relationships, including our ability to sympathize with others.

LIVING WITH ANGER
by Myra Chave-Jones

Takes a positive view of anger and how it can be used as an important part of our lives.

FREE TO FAIL
by Russ Parker

A Christian exploration of the problems many people have with facing up to failure and its place in the spiritual life.

SEVEN FOR A SECRET THAT'S NEVER BEEN TOLD
Healing the wounds of sexual abuse in childhood
by Tracy Hansen

A moving account of a survivor of child sexual abuse working through the trauma induced by the return of repressed memories.

IMPOSSIBLE DECISIONS
Making decisions when no way seems right
by Doreen Padfield, with Deborah Padfield

A down-to-earth look at decisions where, whatever we do, someone will be hurt. The book finds common features in routine choices as well as major dilemmas.

FROM WHERE I SIT
Living with disability in an able-bodied world
by Alison Davis

A disturbing, personal and often funny account of what it is really like to be disabled.

WHO'S THIS SITTING IN MY PEW?
Mentally handicapped people in the church
by Faith Bowers

Considers what the church can do for mentally handicapped people and what they bring to the church.

BEGINNING WHERE I AM
Meditations for young people
by Godfrey Holmes

Meditations and prayers for a wide range of modern situations, with suggestions for beginning your own prayer life.

TRI∧NGLE

Books
can be obtained from
all good bookshops.
In case of difficulty,
or for a complete list of our books,
contact:
SPCK Mail Order
36 Steep Hill
Lincoln
LN2 1LU
(tel: 0522 527 486)